ISBN 978-1-330-27838-3
PIBN 10011036

1 MONTH OF
FREE
READING

at

www.ForgottenBooks.com

By purchasing this book you are eligible for one month membership to ForgottenBooks.com, giving you unlimited access to our entire collection of over 700,000 titles via our web site and mobile apps.

To claim your free month visit:

www.forgottenbooks.com/free11036

English
Français
Deutsche
Italiano
Español
Português

www.forgottenbooks.com

Mythology Photography **Fiction**
Fishing Christianity **Art** Cooking
Essays Buddhism Freemasonry
Medicine **Biology** Music **Ancient
Egypt** Evolution Carpentry Physics
Dance Geology **Mathematics** Fitness
Shakespeare **Folklore** Yoga Marketing
Confidence Immortality Biographies
Poetry **Psychology** Witchcraft
Electronics Chemistry History **Law**
Accounting **Philosophy** Anthropology
Alchemy Drama Quantum Mechanics
Atheism Sexual Health **Ancient History**
Entrepreneurship Languages Sport
Paleontology Needlework Islam
Metaphysics Investment Archaeology
Parenting Statistics Criminology
Motivational

A TREATISE ON
EMBROIDERY

WITH TWENTY COLOR ILLUSTRATIONS
FROM ORIGINAL MODELS

EDITION DE LUXE   Art Needlework Series Number 8

This book is arranged for the
use of those who desire a more
thorough understanding of the
art of embroidering with silk, and
as a guide for those who may
wish to teach.

Descriptive List of the

VARIOUS ART NEEDLE=WORK SILKS PRODUCED BY

M. HEMINWAY & SONS SILK CO.

Are all of the Celebrated Oriental Dyes, Insuring Permanency and Brilliancy after Laundering.

Japan Floss.—The finest size thread made and one that is universally used for flower work, where close shading is required.

Spanish Floss.—About double size of Japan Floss. The silk is especially suited for scallop work on doilies and centre pieces, and is also recommended for cross-stitching on conventional designs—it is not too heavy for shading large petals, and is preferred by some embroiderers to accomplish quick results, where close shading is not an important feature.

Turkish Floss.—A very glossy silk about double size of Spanish Floss soft twist. The effects produced with this floss have all the beauty of Japan Floss. Applicable for large designs on heavy materials for sofa cushions and table covers.

Twisted Embroidery.—A practical heavy embroidery thread, firmly twisted, suitable for embroidering flannel and all general work where a floss silk is not required. Adapted for button-hole stitch on edge of linen centre pieces.

Japan Outline Silk.—A fine size twisted embroidery silk for outlining and button-holing on infants' sacques and underwear.

Japan Cordinet Silk.—Reverse twist from Japan Outline Silk, made in white for Honiton lace work.

Rope Silk.—Very heavy size embroidery silk; suited for large scroll designs on heavy materials.

Mount Mellick Silk.—Made in pure white and blue white, four sizes: FF, G, H, HH, the latter heavier and harder twist than Rope Silk.

Introduction.

In presenting our series No. 8 Treatise on Embroidery, it has been our aim to give as much variety as possible in the limited space allotted. The pages on stitchery will be found most complete, many additions being made to the most popular stitches shown in our last book, and all so clearly pictured, but little explanation accompanies the illustrations.

In the twenty color plates, the best possible results have been secured, perfection is rarely attained. It is impossible to give natural coloring in any particular flower, only general tone, and the "subtle gradations" so difficult in painting, cannot be expressed in photographic proofs from hand embroidery.

The Opportunity of the Needlewoman.

In the preparation of this book the writer has constantly had in mind the importance of making the instructions so plain and the illustrations so clearly defined, that any lady may by close application, be able to execute without trouble all the handsome examples of art work shown herein. Should any difficulty be experienced, and a teacher of embroidery not be convenient to consult, the publishers of this book will cheerfully, through the correspondence department, give any information desired. ˋ

Many ladies earn a competence by giving embroidery lessons and selling materials to embroidery workers.

One who is able to give instructions in stitches, can with a little exertion organize a paying class of pupils. The work indeed might be enlarged to embrace plain sewing, knitting, crocheting and mending. Attention is particularly directed to pages 79, 80, 81, 82, 83, 84, 85, where are illustrated several small novelties suitable for Christmas, Easter, Birthday gifts, or Whist and Euchre prizes.

For much of the material which has entered into the composition of this book, the publishers are indebted to Miss Grace A. Luther.

Embroidery Hoops.

Rings of embroidery hoops should be frequently rewrapped. It is not unusual to see hoops in the hands of apparently dainty women so dirty they are a disgrace to her cleanliness, not to speak of the ruinously black lines they leave on the work.

The best covering for hoops is a very thin tape about an inch wide, wound so that one edge just barely laps over the other. As a whole bolt of tape may be bought for a few cents, there is absolutely no excuse for dingy coverings.

The silver rings in vogue several years ago are really not very practical. If wrapped, they had much better be wood, and if unwrapped, the inevitable tarnishing, unless the greatest care is exercised, will leave ugly stains on delicate materials.

The two parts of the embroidery hoops should fit so tightly that a certain amount of pressure must be exerted to fit them together after the work is spread on them. Fit the work smoothly over the lower ring before putting on the top. If there is the slightest wrinkle, or the work sags, the effect is much worse than if no hoops were used.

Attention is directed to the "Practical" Oblong Embroidery Hoop, illustrated on page 16.

How to Press Embroidery.

Work done on a frame is usually straighter and less apt to be puckered than that done over the fingers; but even then fine linen will often draw a little under close embroidery unless done by a skilled workwoman. If the embroidered article you wish to press be of linen, use a table or board made soft by two thicknesses of blankets and covered with a clean white cloth. Lay your work upon it, wrong side up, and be careful to keep the edges very straight. Dampen a sponge and rub gently over the article until it is quite damp, and press with a hot iron, which should be most carefully tested to see that it will not scorch, and also that it is absolutely clean and smooth. If there is any uncertainty about the condition of the iron put a damp cloth over the embroidery and press through that.

Embroidery done with floss or silk should be kept as neat as possible, so that washing may not be necessary at first, as there is danger of the embroidery becoming roughtened and the threads pulling. Work done on silk or satin must be pressed with a cooler iron than on linen, for it is more liable to scorch—and besides some colors of silk fabric may fade from *too great heat*. It cannot be dampened, either, as that would stiffen the silk; but if the embroidery is heavy, and the work puckered badly, the embroidery itself may be moistened slightly. Always remember to press on the wrong side.

How to Distinguish Chemically Bleached Linen from Grass Bleached.

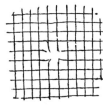

Fig 1

Really excellent hemstitching cannot be done on poor linen. The better the linen the better the design and durability of the hemstitching. When the threads of the linen are strong and round, the stitching will be clear and well defined; when the threads are angular, weak and uneven, the stitching cannot be artistic nor permanent. This applies to embroidery also. The quality of the linen depends upon the manner in which it is prepared. The process of bleaching flax by chemicals is much cheaper and quicker than that of bleaching by exposure to the air. But the fibres are weakened by the acids, frequently oxalic acid, used in the process of bleaching. The grass bleaching does not impair the quality of the fibres. Grass bleaching is more expensive, because it takes more time and requires more care, but the difference between the two is not more than one or two cents a yard for the embroidery linens.

The large sale of the chemically bleached linens is due as much to the lack of knowledge as to the cheap prices and a whiter shade. An examination and comparison of the two qualities of linens, the round thread art linens with the chemically bleached art linens under a microscope, shows that the needle cutting

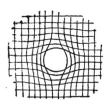

Fig. 2

through the chemically bleached, leaves broken and ragged threads like the first illustration herewith; while a puncture of the needle in the grass bleached, round thread linens, shows that the needle has simply separated the threads by passing between them, as in illustration Fig. 2. In one case the threads are bent; in the other the threads are broken. The fibres of the chemically bleached linens are uneven, brittle and inferior, while the fibres of the grass bleached linens are practically unimpaired, so that when the needle is withdrawn and the cloth rubbed and pulled, the threads of the latter resume their former position, and the cloth will be as good as ever.

For Table of Contents
See Page 98

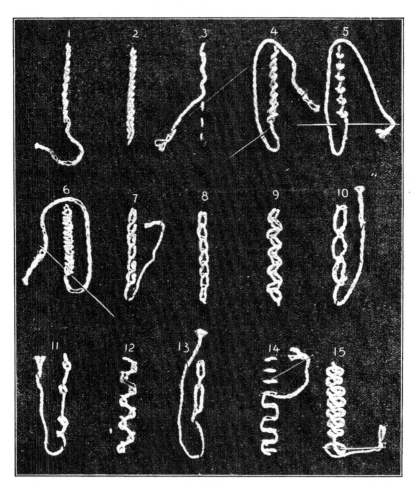

PLATE NO. I.

Steps in Stitchery.

Description of stitches illustrated at *Plate I.*

1. *Outline Stitch.*—Work from left to right on line to be embroidered. Bring needle to right side of fabric, take stitch of required length, bringing the needle back, with a back stitch, to right side of fabric, midway and close to the left side of first stitch. Repeat indefinitely. Stitches must be of equal length and needle always brought up on the same side of each succeeding stitch. Some workers insure an even line by bringing the needle when finishing the back stitch, out from the same hole pierced when forming the last stitch. Length of stitch naturally depends upon the size of silk employed.

2. *Thick Outline Stitch.*—Proceed as above, save that stitches are carried at an angle across the line to be embroidered, instead of directly on it. This stitch when wide, is slanted satin stitch.

3. *Twisted Outline* or *Reverse Couching,* consists of evenly run stitches following the given line. A second thread is wound back on the surface by passing under each stitch. It is well to use the head of the needle when passing under the running.

4. *Cable Stitch* or *Twisted Chain.*—The illustration is the least confusing instruction for this very useful stitch. From this we see that when thread and needle are brought to the surface, the thread is held down with the thumb of the left hand, the needle is then slantingly inserted at right of thread, brought out at left, and pulled through. The second stitch repeats the process, the needle being inserted on a line and to the right of the finish of last stitch.

5. *Beading Snail Trail* or *Knotted Outline.*—It may be made exactly like the last, only with longer intervals between stitches, or else the needle may be passed under straight, from right to left, instead of at an angle. See illustration.

6. *Raised Rope Outline* is also the same stitch, the needle inserted at an angle and immediately beneath the foregoing stitch.

7. *Broken Chain Cording* is made by holding down the thread with thumb, inserting needle just below and to right of starting point. Bring out needle about an ⅛ inch below and in line with starting point, pull through, forming loop. Repeat, inserting needle to right and outside of loop.

8. *Chain Stitch* commenced as above but needle is inserted in same hole as starting point, that is, inside of loop.

9. *Zigzag Chain.*—Same as above, save that needle is inserted at an alternating angle instead of up and down.

10. *Knot* and *Chain Stitch* is made very large in the cut to illustrate the method. In commencing, having brought thread to right side of fabric, hold it down with thumb. Place point of needle to left, under silk so held, and twist in a loop. Insert at right of silk and bring out again ¼ inch below and in line with starting point. This forms a long loop with a tight coil at top. Again hold silk, twist loop and insert to right and outside of last loop.

11. *Knot Drop* or *Gordian Knot Stitch* somewhat resembles beaded outline at first glance. The method is quite different however. Bring silk to right side of fabric and hold down with thumb. Pass point of needle under

PLATE NO. 2.

and over silk from left to right and take up small stitch on outline, throw silk to left, around point of needle and draw taut. Make second knot ¼ inch below first.

12. *Double Beading* commenced like No. 5 but worked in zigzag line. When the silk is held down for the right hand knot, the needle is inserted slightly downward from right to left. For left hand knot, it is inserted from left to right.

13. *Link Stitch* is a variation of chain stitch. The first link is made like No. 8, when the thread is brought to the right side of the fabric at base of link, it is held down and the needle passed under and over it in the manner of No. 11 and inserted ⅛ inch below the base of first link, to be brought out again, in a straight line ¼ inch below. Here throw thread to the left, thus forming a large and a small link. See illustration.

14. *Scaling Stitch* shows a line of parallel straight stitches. A second thread winds over these, scaling from one line to the next.

15. *Heminway Cable Stitch.*—The illustration amply instructs in this stitch which analysis shows to be the knot drop stitch slightly modified. The stitch taken, after winding thread around needle, is longer and at right angles to stamping line,—that is the sole difference.

Description of stitches illustrated at *Plate 2*

1. *Loop Bullion Stitch.* Bring silk to right side of fabric, insert needle again as near as possible and take up ⅛ inch stitch. Now wind silk around needle (as shown in illustration) about ten times and draw through, holding

the coils in place as needle and silk run through them. The length of coils made being greater than the stitch the bullion is looped. Bullion stitch requires a little practice to ascertain how tight to wind and hold the silk.

2. *Double Bullion* is simply two bullion stitches placed side by side and slanted, alternating groups slanting in the same direction. Wheat bullion is double bullion with two groups placed close together at their bases, and slanting away from each other at top, following the formation of wheat.

3. A central outline with bird's eye stitches each side.

4. *Line Couching.*—A desired number of strands is brought through from the wrong side and held while a single strand holds them in place by means of seed stitches at regular intervals.

BULLION STITCH

5. *Cat Stitch.*

6. *Bullion Box Stitch* is made by placing bullion stitches as indicated in the illustration and then finishing with the cross and straight stitches seen at centre and sides.

5. *Cat Stitch.*

6. *Bullion Box Stitch* is made by placing bullion stitches as indicated in the illustration and then finishing with the cross and straight stitches seen at centre and sides.

7. *Zigzag Knot and Chain,* combined with French knots makes a decoration stitch. (Compare No. 10, Plate I.)

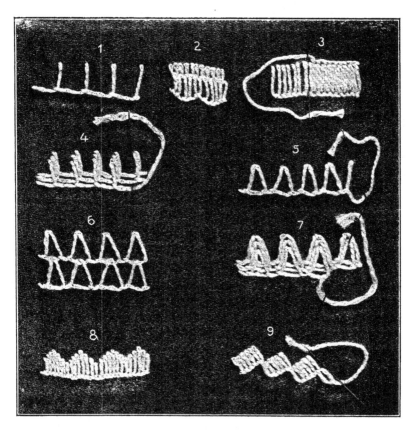

PLATE NO. 3.

8. A development of two stitches already described. The three steps in its development may be seen in the details illustrated. After the silk is brought to the right side, it is held down, the needle point is slipped under and over the silk from left to right, inserted close to starting point and brought out a quarter of an inch below, forming a loop indentical with No. 10, Plate I. The silk is then carried to the right, held down and ¼ inch from base of loop a short stitch is taken up from left to right under the held down thread. See a. Here we had No. 5, Plate I. Next this last stitch made through the central loop, see b, then again ¼ inch to the left. The stitch is repeated for a 3d time. Now holding down the thread, insert the needle just below the central loop, bringing out ¼ inch below, this last is a repitition of the first made loop.

9. *Rosebud Bullion* needs no description to anyone familiar with bullion stitch.

10. Commence as in No. 8, then fasten down the base of first loop with small seed stitch, bring out the needle in a line and ¼ below. From here make an upward pointed bird's eye finishing just below the first with its seed stitch passing over the base of first loop. Bring out the needle at beginning of bird's eye stitch, and make two more of them, one to right and one to left. Repeat from beginning.

11. *Satin Stitch.*

12. *Whipping.*—This stitch must be worked over a double line of run stitches placed for filling along an outline, then work over and over, taking up as small a stitch as possible on the needle. Some people merely hold strands on the surface for filling instead of running them in but it is far more difficult to maintain an even line when working in this manner.

13. *V Stitch.*—Bring thread to right side of fabric, hold down, insert needle ¼ inch to right, bring out in centre and a trifle below, insert again, making a seed stitch, which holds in place and forms the V, repeat. This stitch may also be used for surface covering stitch, if lines are repeated close together, or succeeding lines may be worked in opposite directions, the Vs fitting in between each other.

Description of stitches illustrated at *Plate 3.*

1. *Blanket Stitch.*

2. *Double Buttonhole.*—A second row of buttonhole stitches is placed between those of the first. They may form a shell or plain edge.

3. *Ribbon Stitch.*—Two rows of buttonhole stitches are placed opposite each other, stitch between stitch—see illustration. The buttonhole stitches may be close together, or separated. When close together the work looks like satin stitch with an outlined edge.

4. *Fence Stitch* shows succeeding rows of buttonhole stitches worked each just below and a little to the left of the last.

5. *Tent Buttonhole* is simple buttonhole slanted, as illustrated.

6. A Surface Stitch formed of the above.

7. An attractive development of No. 5 formed by placing succeeding rows close below each other.

8. *Pointed Buttonhole.*

9. *Box Buttonhole.*

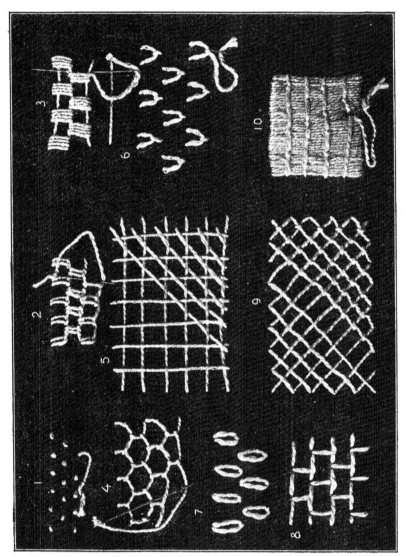

PLATE NO. 4.

Description of stitches illustrated at *Plate* 4.

Plate 4 illustrates simple and useful stitches for surface covering. A frame or hoop should always be used when covering surfaces.

No. 1 is *seeding,* which is merely short, even back stitches placed at regular intervals, succeeding lines having the back or seed stitch midway between and of adjudged distance below the seeds of preceding line.

2. *Buttonhole bricking* shows groups of two close buttonhole stitches separated by intervals. Stitches of succeeding lines fall naturally in these intervals.

3. *Satin blocks* are worked over parallel lines of stitches as shown by illustration.

4. *Honey comb stitch* consists of a row of short, separated buttonhole stitches. A second row has its stitches placed midway between and a little below those above, thus pulling the thread down in a point. Each row proceeds in like manner. The stitch must be regular and not so tight as to pucker the foundation.

5. *Single caning* shows a frame-work of evenly spaced horizontal and vertical stitches forming squares. The silk is then woven diagonally through these. If the needle is invariably passed *under* the under cross bar and *over* the upper, there will be no mistake in the interlacing. Diagonals may be run in both directions if desired, and in this case the effect is very pretty if carried out in two shades of silk, one for cross bars and one for diagonals.

6. *V or scale stitch* may be placed as close together as desired.

7. *Teardrop* is bird's eye stitch placed in rows, and is most effective when stitches are placed midway between spaces of preceding row.

8. *Brick stitch* shows a long stitch on right side and short one on wrong. The second row has upright stitching ending between long stitches. If preferred these uprights may be slanted instead of straight, but all stitches must be even, and if slanting stitches are used they must be all at same angle.

9. The upper left hand portion of No. 9 illustrates SURFACE DARNING. Stitches laid in one direction are crossed by others at right angles and are woven under one and over the next. The lower corner illustrates diaper couching. An even cross bar is first made as for caning. The threads are then caught down with a seed stitch at each intersection. Seed stitches may run up and down or crosswise, as shown. They may also form a cross if desired. Two colors are generally employed for couching, one for crossbars and one for seed stitches.

10. *Solid couching* shows the surface covered with satin stitches. Stitches cross these at regular intervals, these may be single, as illustrated, or in groups. These are in turn caught down with seed stitches.

PLATE NO. 5.

Description of stitches illustrated at *Plate* 5.

Plate 5 illustrates developments of feather stitch, buttonhole and various combinations of fancy stitches, all easily understood from the reproductions.

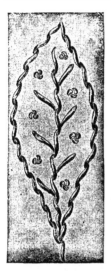

Outline—Feather and
French Knot
Stitches.

A Page of Stitches Suitable for Mount Mellick Designs.

Chain Stitch with Net
Stitch Centre.

Double Outline with
Herring Bone
Centre.

Pyramid Stitch.

Conventional Feather

Everywhere, and on all styles of garments, from whole costumes to separate pieces of lingerie, we find at present the very popular eyelet work figuring as the chief decoration.

It has the charm of extreme simplicity, both in design and workmanship, but herein lies a serious pitfall for the careless or unwary worker. The very simplicity of the method of execution leaves no chance for concealing defects in complications of curves and stitches; therefore, it must be most carefully done.

The implements required are a medium-sized needle, a pair of sharp-pointed scissors, an embroidery hoop and a stiletto. Though the hoop is recommended, better and quicker results can be obtained without a hoop.

Heminway's "Practical" Embroidery Hoop

The designs usually consist of groups of oval and round disks, so arranged as to form circles, festoons, wreaths, etc., and these are occasionally embellished by insertions of point d'esprit or Brussels net, when the openings are large enough to warrant it.

A pretty addition to such work is the introduction of the filled satin stitch, or what really constitutes French laid work; and with a buttonholed edge a quite elaborate piece of embroi-

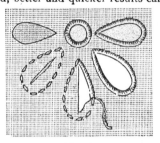

Fig. A

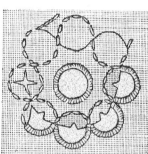

Fig. B

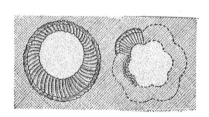

Fig. C
Detail of Eyelet Work

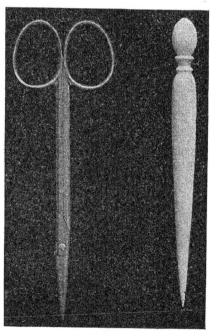

Stiletto and Scissors

dery may be evolved.

This style of decoration is particularly well adapted to stocks, collars, shoulder capes, shirt-waist sets and flouncings for skirts. Eyelet work is exceedingly durable, and if well done will last a lifetime. In proof of this many women can show fine examples of the work which are the handiwork of their grandmothers, for a generation or two ago it was almost the only style of fancy work indulged in during leisure hours.

The cuts herewith shown indicate quite plainly the various steps in the process. Almost anyone can draw a design in pencil on the silk or linen selected for the work, although it is generally preferable to have it stamped.

The work is held in the left hand while the right hand follows the pattern with the needle. The Heminway "Practical" oblong hoop is the most satisfactory one to use for solid work. The first step consists only in outlining the pattern with a plain running stitch, such as is used in ordinary sewing. The material is cut inside each oval or circle, from one end to the other, so that the last step in the process may more easily be accomplished. This is done by folding back on the wrong side the

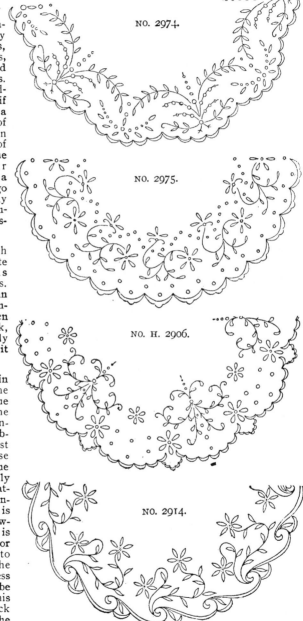

NO. 2974.

NO. 2975.

NO. H. 2906.

NO. 2914.

clipped edges of the material with the needle, while the opening thus formed is overhanded with a very snort, close, slanting stitch. Care must be taken to hold the fabric stretched according to the thread, or else the openings will be misshapen and the work drawn in effect, and satisfactory laundering will be impossible.

The plain outline stitch is the one usually used for all worked stems. The best results in eyelet-work, when done in silk, will be obtained by using either *Spanish* or *Turkish floss,* both of which, as made by M. Heminway & Sons, are beautifully adapted to this work. A heavier effect, especially in outline, may be secured by the substitution of *Twisted Embroidery Silk,* but this is only desirable in large patterns, where a heavy silk will add to the general effect. The wide variety of shades in which these silks can be obtained affords the embroiderer unlimited range of choice in the selection of colors where vivid combinations are preferred to white or subdued tones.

Button-Hole Stitch.

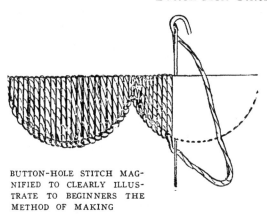

BUTTON-HOLE STITCH MAG-
NIFIED TO CLEARLY ILLUS-
TRATE TO BEGINNERS THE
METHOD OF MAKING

This stitch is used in working scallops in French embroidery on silk, flannel, linen, and cotton fabrics, and also to finish outlines on Roman and appliqué embroidery.

In using the button-hole stitch to work scalloped edges the scallop should first be filled in, to give it a raised effect, beside adding to the durability of the edge.

In filling, use coarse white embroidery or darning cotton. The chain is a good stitch to fill in the edge of scallop, making as many

BUTTON-HOLE STITCH.   (FILLED)

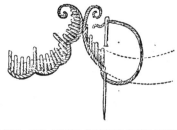

LONG AND SHORT BUTTON-HOLE STITCH

rows as width of scallop. This will give the scallop a heavy, rich, and raised effect. The needle should pass through the material just at the edge of the

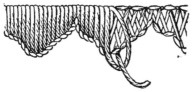

top thread, coming out under the lower line, while the thread is held by the left thumb, a little to the right of where the needle is to come through, so that as the needle is drawn up a loop is formed which fastens itself. In making button-hole outline for Roman embroidery, the stitch is usually worked over a German cord; and in articles where the

RAISED BUTTON-HOLE STITCH

Basket Stitch.

frequently called Persian and "Janina," is useful for filling long, narrow petals or spaces in conventional designs. It is simply a crossed stitch. Beginning a little to the left of tip of petal, bring the needle up through, pass it downward to the right across at the back, up at a point opposite where it went down, then across the first thread, up to the point nearly opposite where it first came out. The stitches may be wide apart or close, as required, and the petal is finished by outlining.

BASKET STITCH

Bird's-Eye Stitch.

Which may be used for small, narrow petals, as those of the star-flower, marguerite, etc., is a sort of chain stitch, starting from the centre. Put the needle up through, then down again and out in a long stitch to the tip of the petal, bring it up inside the loop of silk, and putting it down again just outside, forming a short stitch to hold the petal in place.

PETALS IN BIRD'S-EYE STITCH

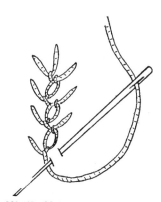

MOUNT MELLICK BRIAR STITCH

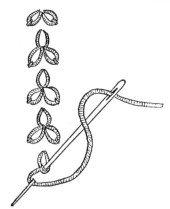

CLOVER-LEAF CHAIN STITCH

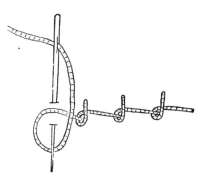

SNAIL STITCH

WEAVING STITCH
Leaves, Long and Short

Instructions for Padding

All Strawberry, Cherry, Holly, Grape and turned over petals should first be padded to give them the raised effect.

Method—First fill in with soft *white* darning cotton, putting all the filling on top, using the short stitch underneath. This is to avoid having the work too thick, which would cause trouble in washing.

The stitches should run in an opposite direction to what you are going to embroider; otherwise, the silk would sink into the cotton and it would take twice as much time and silk to cover.

The stitch used for padding is a long back stitch taken just inside of the stamping. Be sure to use the short stitch underneath.

FRENCH KNOT STITCH

French Knot Stitch.

Is used for the centres of such flowers as the daisy, for the anthers of others, for golden-rod and such as are formed of masses of tiny blossoms. The needle is brought up at the exact spot where the knot is to be. Hold the silk in left hand, twist it around the needle, once, twice, three times, or more, according to size of knot required, then pass the needle through the fabric close to the point where it came up, drawing it down with the right hand, and with the thumb of the left keeping the twists in place until the knot is secure.

SOLID KENSINGTON STITCH

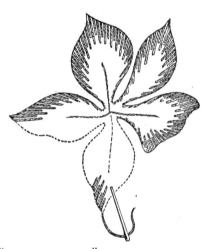

"LONG AND SHORT" KENSINGTON STITCH

Kensington Stitch.

First put the linen in a tight-fitting hoop or frame, having the work "tight as a drum." Start the outer edge of the flower with two strands of Japan Floss, or one of Spanish or Turkish Floss, either working the "over and over" long and short stitch, or else taking the needle under the linen and carrying it to the top of design. By this method you can keep the shape of the petals and cover the stamping. After the outer edge is finished use one strand to shade, working toward you until the petal is finished. With the work in a frame you can use both hands, putting the needle· in with the right, drawing it out with the left.

Raised Rope Outline.

Very handsome in heavy silk; method of making shown, and the stitch can be varied by making the stitches which cross rather smaller and farther apart. There is but the one thread as shown; it is brought out at the top of the line along which the work is to be done, and the first stitch is made in the same way as the last shown.

RAISED ROPE OUTLINE

Raised Satin Stitch.

Is worked in the same way as satin stitch, the surface of the fabric being first "padded" as shown. The "jewels" in embroidery of recent years are made in this way.

RAISED SATIN STITCH

Split Stitch.

Split stitch is worked like the ordinary outline or stem stitch, except that the needle is always brought up through the silk, which is thus split; it is used for delicate outlines, and the effect is somewhat that of a chain stitch, not well defined.

SPLIT OUT-
LINE STITCH.

Parts of a Flower.

It is quite essential, when a flower is to be embroidered, that the worker should possess a knowledge of its different parts, and their relation to each other.

The illustration will show these distinct parts, with their individual sections or divisions.

The *corolla* is the blossom or flower portion, and is often in a single section, having edges more or less open and convoluted, as in the morning-glory, petunia, lily, etc.

When the corolla is divided, as in case of wild rose, poppy, violet, pansy, etc., each of these divisions is a *petal*.

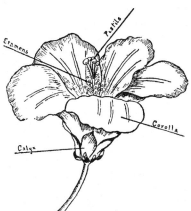

FLOWER PARTS.

The green bud enclosing lower portion of corolla is the *calyx,* which, like the corolla, is often in one sheath-like piece, with edge more or less open or pointed. When the calyx is divided each section so formed is a *sepal.* The sepals unite at a point near their union with stem or continue separately to the stem, as in the rose and other flowers.

The *stamen* in centre of flower consists of an *anther,* or fertilizing part, borne on a stem called the *filament.* The pistil is the part containing the seed vessels, and this varies in number with the nature of the flower.

The natural grain of a petal is toward the centre or calyx, and this grain should be carefully preserved. The direction of turned-over petals, etc., may easily be ascertained by cutting from a piece of paper, or drawing, a petal to be worked, stroking this with the slant or grain of natural petal, and by turning over the edge to be copied in whatever direction is called for. The stitches will lie clearly as they should be worked, and this method will be found very satisfactory and reliable.

An effort has been made herein to obviate the necessity for reference to other sources for information as to the essential points and details of flower painting with the needle, and it is thought that in these pages the embroideress, whether amateur or expert, will find a clear *because* to her every *why.*

Chrysanthemum Decoration.

Descriptive of Color Plate No. 6.

The Chrysanthemum is a flower which lends itself readily to embroidery. In the color plate we have an example wrought in exquisitely natural coloring in the following shades of Japan Floss.

Flowers.—Pinks—1657, 540, 541, 330, 331, 333, 334, 389. Yellows—361, 362.

Foliage.—Greens—371 to 375. Browns—229, 230E, 230¾, 304.

With the proper color gradations at hand the curving of the stitchery in the sinuous petals demands our first attention.

A chain stitch cotton padding is placed at the tips of petals before embroidering. This in no case extends more than ¼-inch, generally a single line suffices. Where size permits, commence with two strands of silk, shading in with one in the large flower. The tips of outer petals are mainly pale pink, 540, 541 and 330. Shade in stronger toward the centre, giving care to shape the stitches to the sinuous curves of the petals. Occasional stitches of yellow 362 will give good effect. Lower petals are begun with deeper shades 541 and 331. Some few show 333 on top and these last shade lighter toward the centre. Inner petals are all pale, tipped with 361 yellow, into which is shaded 1657, 540, 541 in various petals. Fill in back of these petals with 333 to throw them in relief. The opening flower and bud are also padded in these darker tones 333, 334 and 389 predominating as may be seen.

The stems are of 373, 374 and 375 greens, with which is dashed a little 304 and 230E brown. Leaves shade darker from the tips. The highest leaf in plate is commenced with two strands of 372, while 372½ shades into this with 374 to right of middle vein and 229 brown on the left. The vein is a single strand of 374. Same shades appear in the turned portion of next large leaf, the under portion of which is worked with 373, 374 green and 230E brown.

2981C.

Chrysanthemum Center

Design No. 2981c.

Sizes :—12, 18, 22 and 27 inches.

Materials.—M. Heminway & Sons' Japan Floss for floral decoration and Turkish Floss for scallop.

Flowers.—Yellows—Line 360 to 368 or A645 to 653. Pinks— Line 580 to 588 or 330 to 334.

Foliage.—Greens—Line 512 to 516 or Line 370 to 375. Browns—301 or 302.

Scallop. — White — No. 691. Couch seven · strands of pale green above buttonholing, fastening down with darker shade. For Pink Chrysanthemum use lightest shades for edge of top petals ; darker toward stem. Touch outer and lighter petals with Yellow, A645, using this shade lightly and with care, a suggestion only of Yellow tip being desired. In some petals in other flowers shadow Green 0682 may be used. This applies, too, to Yellow flowers, which are also tipped with White, 688. Start petals, when broad enough not to be heavy or clumsy, with two strands of Japan Floss, subsequent shadings with one.

The stitches must be very carfully curved to form of petals, which are dis_ tinctly marked. All have a common direction—that of base of flower, and their intentions should not be frustrated by improperly directed thread.

The foliage is worked in ˌtwo lines of Greens, which adds considerably to the shading, and relieves the subject of the flat monotonous repetition so obvious in the majority of work of this character.

For leaves, use two strands of the lightest Green on outer edge of most prominent leaves, shading with one strand. The leaves lying in shadow are begun with second, shading with darker numbers. An occasional tint of Brown, 301 or 302, on tip of old leaf or along edges or a spot in centre, adds naturalness and a suggestion of the early autumn's touch, so welcome with these flowers. About two, or in largest petals, three, shades of color will be found sufficient, although this may be largely a matter of individual taste. The calyxes are in Light Green on tip and edges, shading deeper toward stems, which are worked in light shades also, approximating as nearly as possible the cool Gray-Green of the natural stem so familiar to all. While a cold and brilliant flower in itself, its careful treatment and arrangement of color and accessories, afford a harmonious and graceful decoration which assures its popularity.

Biedermaier Embroidery.

Design No. 794.

Sizes: 12, 18, 22 and 27 inch.

M. Heminway & Sons' Turkish Floss.—Gray—1196, 1200, 1202. Red—0655, 655, 657, 658, 659. Green—370, 371, 372, 372½, 373, 374, 375. Blue—671, 671½. *Twisted Embroidery.*—White—691.

DESIGN NO. 794.

As its name designates, Biedermaier Embroidery is of German origin, and although but a revival of old time methods, is enjoying a vogue not readily attained by absolutely new comers in the field of needlework. Its designs are the outcome of Empire suggestions, simplified and without the cold formality of the former, so that they carry with them a very homelike atmosphere, and one that is particularly suitable to the present development of house furnishing on simple lines. We see the motives of wreathes and garlands, so familiar in the Empire style, made quaintly attractive by additional prim little trees and flowers drawn on conventional lines. Little silhouettes of our grandmother's times are also frequently pictured together with ladies of dainty stateliness in enormous pokes and voluminous beruffled skirts. All these are part and parcel of this unusual form of decoration. The color is no less a feature than the motives of design and we work with bright tints and strong contrasts, but invariably toned with black or softened with dull blues and greens, so that the scheme, though bright, is never garish.

The centerpiece shown, No. 794, is a very characteristic design, and illustrates the whimsical bits of ornament which constitute the units and basis of Biedermaier. In it we have formal little flower trees growing from sturdy tubs, of gray, with baskets of odd roses, and connecting the two is a soft blue-gray ribbon suspending Empire wreathes and what is called a "swag" in decorative parlance; a term applied to a pendant or festooned garlands of leaves and flowers.

All Biedermaier stitching is simple satin stitch and simple thick upright outline stitches and French Knots—these are about all which are brought into play. Padding is of too occasional nature to form one of the features of the needlework. Turkish Floss of M. Heminway & Sons is the proper medium for this embroidery.

Description.—In the design illustrated, flower tints are carried out in shades of gray 1196, 1200 and 1202. The tub has an outline of the medium shade, and a second of the palest shade leaves a space which is filled in with French Knots of the darkest tone. Long rows of straight stitches of this last fill in the center portion of the tub. Balls of red 658 and 659 give a touch of brightness to the otherwise sombre scheme. The same tones appear in the basket which utilizes thick upright outlines for its top, base and support. The top requires shade 1200, the base 1196, the legs 1202. The weaving of the basket is done in a sort of diaper couching, the couching in 1196 being a small cross over the intersecting long stitches of 1202. Between the couching crosses are French Knots of 1200. The foliage shades dark to light as it ascends from baskets and flower tubs. The rose leaves of trees and baskets show shading from 370 to 375, the intervening gradations numbering 371, 372, 372½ and 374. The rose tree stem begins with 373 and works into 375 at its base. The same tints are required in the wreaths which are darkest near the ribbon and shade to the palest green at the tips. Flowers on trees present darkest blossoms toward the top, three shades in sequences being used in each flower. Beginning at the tops, these run in the following order—659, 658, 657, the next flower shading is composed of 658, 657. 655 and the third set of 657, 655 and 0655. The three roses in the basket call for 655, 657, 658 and 659 with the largest flower executed in 655, 657 and 658 in the centre of the group. The gray blue ribbons require shades 671 and 671½. A scallop in 691 Twist Embroidery finishes the embroidery of this effective piece which is made more ornamental by an outer edging of Irish lace. Plate doilies may be had to match the centerpiece.

IMPORTANT.

To intelligently follow the embroidery lessons in the book don't fail to secure of dealers a sample card showing the silk itself in every shade made in all sizes of silk threads. See illustration on page 85.

BIEDERMAIER PILLOW.

Pillow Design No. 800/1

Stamped on cream Bavarian Linen, embroidered in Turkish Floss after style suggested in centerpiece article preceding.

EYELET EMBROIDERY AND ITS FUTURE POSSIBILITIES

Series No. 7

A book of thirty pages, size 8 x 11 inches, containing eighty illustrations of useful articles that can be made in Eyelet Embroidery and Hardanger Work with silk.

Published at 25c. Mailed, while the edition lasts, for 6 two-cent stamps.

Address the publishers of this book at their Mills, WATERTOWN, CONN.

Orchid and Ferns Decoration.

Descriptive of Color Plate No. 5

Size of Centerpiece, 25 inch.

Design No. 2935.

M. Heminway & Sons' Japan Floss for floral decorations. Turkish Floss for scallop.

Japan Floss.—Pink—540, 541, 542, 543, 1657, 544, 580. Yellow —409½, 0409. Brown—229, 392, 393, 303. Green—310, 310½, 370, 371, 372, 372½, 373, 374, 375, 480, 481, 482, 483, 484, 485, 486. White—688.

Turkish Floss.—White—691. Pink—1657. Green—310.

NO. 2935.

An orchid and fern decoration is the subject of centre No. 2935, an excellent idea of which is given in color plate 5. Very little padding is used in rendering this design—slightly raise the chalice rim in the orchids and turnovers on the leaves—that will suffice. The necessary slant of Kensington stitches is illustrated by the color plate. The deepest coloring appears about the fluted rim of the flower cup—in all cases it shades lighter and merges into yellow in the interior. The blending of pale pink and green in some flowers gives a charming symphony of opalescence. In working the full face flower, shown in the color plate, use two strands of pink 543 around the chalice rim. Into this, run single threads of 541 and 542, also in the lower portions over this are scattered single long stitches of 545. Yellow 409½, then 0409 appear in the hollow opening. The outside of the chalice is palest under the rim, 540, 541 and 542 are needed for this. The last three also color the remaining three petals, the deepest shade working in where they join the stem. A white orchid is worked with 688, 310 and 310½ greens, and before mentioned yellows. Shade in the green near the stems.

Stems and leaves call for the line 480 to 486. The large leaf in the color plate is tipped with 480 and into this runs a bit of 229 tan. 481, 482, 483 and 484 succeed each other in the leaf—485 and 486 form the dark stems.

Shadings of the line 370 appear in the fern with stems of 303. Turkish Floss is used in the large scallops with a cord of seven strands of 1657 pink couched with 485 green above this. Buttonholing of 1657 forms the fancy shell between the scalloped divisions and 310 green is worked in above this.

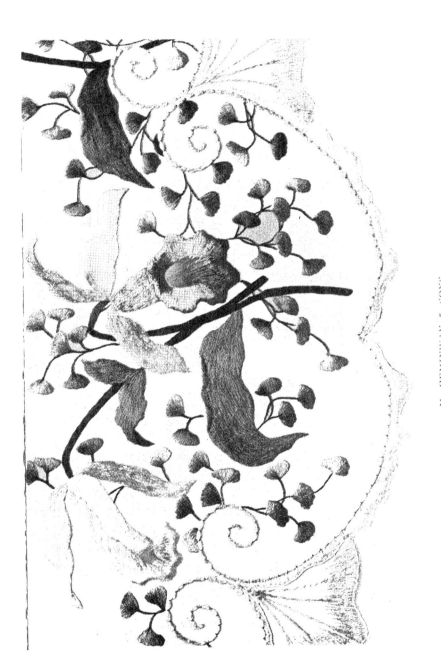

M. HEMINWAY & SONS

ORCHID and FERN....Color Plate No. 5

Reproduced from original models embroidered with

DAMASK DOYLIE, DESIGN NO. 250/1

A Novelty in Damask.

The doylie illustrated is one of four wreath designs woven specially for M. Heminway & Sons Silk Co. and sold to dealers in their silks and art materials.

Three sizes are obtainable: Finger Bowl size about six inches in diameter, Plate size about 12 inches and centerpiece size about 24 inches.

The cut gives but a faint idea of its beauty. The quality of the damask is high grade, pure white linen; the leaves and dots are woven to show clearly and are not to be touched by the needle, the only embroidery being put on the scalloped edge which is closely buttonholed with white Turkish Floss.

The designs obtainable in three sizes are: Clover (also known as Shamrock), Thistle, Double Rose and Holly. This pretty novelty is meeting with a large sale which proves its popularity, particularly among those who have little time for embroidery and are not skillful in executing intricate shadings in flowers.

The prices generally made by dealers are: 12 cents each, for Finger Bowl size; 30 cents each, for Plate size; $1.25 each for centerpiece size.

Box of Strawberries.

Descriptive of Color Plate No. 8.

Shades required.

M. Heminway & Sons' Japan Floss.—Brown—227, 228, 230, 230½, 230¾, 230D, 230E. Red—A655, 0655, 656, 657, 658, 659, 660, 661, 662. Yellow—409½. Green—481, 482, 483, 484, 485. Red Brown—300, 302, 304.

The box of strawberries shows a beautiful and skilful blending of the various shades employed in embroidering this luscious fruit. Each berry presents a different blending and combination of shades and each one is a practical lesson and helpful, giving suggestions which may be applied whenever strawberries are to be embroidered, no matter in what manner of grouping or arrangement. There is a preliminary cotton padding laid in most of the berries of the illustration. This padding must be done with care, the thread laid evenly with a short back stitch, and the use of a frame or hoop is *very necessary.* The padding should run at right angles to the direction of the silk stitching, so that there will be no opportunity for the latter to sink down into the cotton. Where the relief is very high, several layers of this padding will be necessary, the greatest height being reached in the centre of the berry. A detail of padding is given on page 20.

Description.—One strand of Japan Floss should be used in embroidering the berries, the stitches in the illustration running straight down from the top and sides of the berry to the base. This method is more simple than slanting the stitch by working from the edges toward the base, and also seems to better express the texture of the berry. The lighter berries should be shaded from Nos. A655, 0655 and 656 with delicate touches of 657. These are the true tints of the Nova Scotia berries, while deeper shadings are obtained with Nos. 657, 658, 659, 660 and 661, and occasional stitches of No. 662. Yellow Japan Floss No. 409½ is the shade for seeding, and it is with small straight stitches or fine French knots that we express the real fruit of the strawberry plant.

The greens of the strawberry leaves and sepals are soft and varied, and are well expressed by shades Nos. 481, 482, 483, 484 and 485. The large leaf in the illustration is beautifully modelled in these shades, while a skillful use of Red Brown No. 302 suggests the bloom upon the leaf. Subtle coloring of this sort must be sparingly indulged in by the amateur for the line between hodge podge and harmony is very fine, and the delicacy of treatment of apparently opposing shades must not be entrusted to the untrained eye. Red Brown No. 300 is blended with green No. 481 in working the turn over of the leaf, while for veining 302 and red No. 661 are employed—the Brown tint 302 is used throughout save on the darker side of the one leaf shown full face.

The berry box affords an excellent study of smooth, woody texture and no better line of color could be desired. The stitches follow the natural grain of the wood, those of the rim running round, while the sides run from the base of the box to the top. The rim is worked in tan No. 228 with little cracks and nail heads represented by the darker tone No. 230E. Where the sides are pictured as showing along the box top, between the inside and outside rims No. 230½ is employed, the stitches following the grain and direction of the sides, are of course at right angles to those of the rim. No. 227 is the shade for the outside of the box with a little shading of 230½ near the base where the leaf casts a shadow upon it. A suggestion of the grain is given by a few deft stitches in No. 230E.

The bottom of the box is worked with 230½, 230E and 230D—just a little of this last appearing in the deep corner shadow, and blending again into 230E —230 and 228 as the base binds into the far side of the box.

The table shows the blending of 227, 230 and 230¾, but little of the last color being used to represent the deep strong shadows thrown by leaves and berries. The distribution of light and shadow is sometimes a puzzle, and the needleworker will ofttimes be sorely troubled if she commences her work without any definite theory to guide her. In general the light is supposed to fall from the upper lefthand corner of a picture or needle painting, and if this is born in mind, the placing of the shadows will be greatly simplified—their natural position must be underneath and to the right of the various objects pictured.

IMPORTANT.

To intelligently follow the embroidery lessons in this book don't fail to secure of dealers a sample card showing the silk itself in every shade made in all sizes of silk threads. See illustration on page 85.

BOX OF STRAWBERRIES

Color Plate No. 8

Reproduced from original models embroidered with

Strawberry Key.

Materials.—M. Heminway & Sons' Japan Floss.

BERRIES.

Red	2.	Shade No.		1
	4.	"	"	2
	6.	"	"	3
	8½.	"	"	4
	10.	"	"	5
	011.	"	"	6
	015.	"	"	7
Seed ....0432.		"	"	8

BLOSSOMS.

White	691.	Shade No.		9
Green	310.	"	"	10
Pink	1655.	"	"	11
Yellow.....	648.	"	"	13
	649.	"	"	13

STAMENS AND OLD BLOSSOMS.

Yellow ... 409. Shade No. 14

LEAVES.

Greens	0432—A
	432—B
	433—C
	434—D
Veins	435—E
Brown	227—F
	229—G

Strawberry Center.

Design No. 2981F.

Sizes: 12, 18, 22 and 27 inches.

Use Japan Floss of M. Heminway & Sons for decoration and Turkish Floss for scallop on this centre.

Description.—Full instructions regarding strawberries are given in article on color plate see pages 29 and 30. Embroider blossoms with single thread of 688, having very slightly raised the outer edge with cotton filling of chain stitch. Work in 0682 toward the centre to give a transparent greenish cast, stamens should be done with straight stitches of yellow 646, with anthers of French knots 648.

Foliage.—Good coloring for

2981F.

large leaves is shown in color plate; in tender leaves and runners 480, 482 and 483 should predominate. The key also shows coloring and lay of stitches.

. *Scallop*—Turkish Floss.—Green 682.—Buttonholing with couching of 7 strands 1655 pink fastened with 1 strand of 374 green forms an effecting scallop. 691 white may replace 682.

Key to Cornflower, Wild Carrot, Wheat.

CORNFLOWER.

Bluet .... 261. Shade No. 1
              262.   "   " 2
              263.   "   " 3
              264.   "   " 4
Black .... 690.   "   " 5
Yellow .... 0409.   "   " 6

WILD CARROT.

White .... 688. Shade No. 9
Pink .... 1657.   "   " 10
Green .... 310.   "   " 11
              310½.   "   " 12

LEAVES AND STEMS.

CORNFLOWER.

Greens .... 372. Shade A
              372½.   "   B
              373.   "   C
              374.   "   D
Brown .... 230¾.   "   E

WHEAT.

Yellow .... 361. Shade No. 13
              0409.   "   " 6
              409½.   "   " 7
              409.   "   " 8
Leaves 0432 to 434—229, 230, 230D.

WILD CARROT, CORNFLOWER and WHEAT
Color Plate No. 1

Reproduced from original models embroidered with
Permanent Oriental Dyes. Japan Floss

2980C.

Cornflower Centerpiece.

Design No. 2980C.

Sizes: 12, 18, 22, 27 inches.

See Color Plate No. 1. Key on page 32.

Japan Floss.—Blossoms.— Bluets—260, 261, 262, 263 and 264. Line 330 to 335 and 581 to 587. Leaves.—Line 371 to 374.

*Turkish Floss.—*White—691.

The Cornflower or Kaiser Bloom is sometimes called the National flower of Germany, for when the mother of William I was in hiding from the army of Napoleon, she wove garlands of the persistent little blossom, decking her little ones with the gay color in her ef-forts to comfort them as they cried for food, and surely their "royal blue," made them a fitting crown for prince or emperor, and carried a prophetic symbolism.

Description.—Commence the flowers with 2 strands and shade in with one. Refer to key for distribution of shading. The green calyx cup is underlaid with two layers of padding stitches, the first laid crosswise, the second lengthwise. Pad with long stitches all on the right side. Cover with satin stitch run-ning crosswise, and over this spread a lattice of two strands of black 690 caught down with lengthwise stitches at each intersecting point. Use yellow 409 or green 372 for this. In embroidering a number of flowers as on the accompanying centerpiece, No. 2980C, give variety by keeping some blossoms in deep and some in lighter shades. For a dark blossom begin with two strands of 262, work at top of petal, into this work one strand of 263, followed by 264 or 265. For lighter flowers, shade in the same way, only beginning with light tone, 260 or 261. In a profile flower let the petals nearest you be lightest. Flowers in various shades of purplish pinks, or pink and white are seen in nature. These can be worked in among the "bluets," or the entire piece may carry out these unusual tones. The 330 line may be used, as well as selections from 580 line with white 688. For leaves use the 371 line working in Kensington stitch like grass, the length of leaf. Keep the color mainly light, the soft natural effect of bloom is lost when dark tones predomi-nate. The scallop is buttonholed in white Turkish 691.

Wild Carrot Centerpiece.

Design No. 2980B.

Color Plate No. 1

Sizes: 12, 18, 22, 27 inches.

Shades Required

Japan Floss. — White — 688. Greens—0432, 433, 434, 428 to 431. Pinks—1655, 1657. Yellow—645. Browns—229, 230.

Turkish Floss.—White—691.

The fascinating flower clusters of the wild carrot shown at Color Plate No. 1 are details of an extremely pretty and unusual centerpiece pattern. Wild carrot, called by some. Queens Lace, is so rarely seen in embroidery that it must attract special attention, and the design referred to is

2980B.

one of unique daintiness. The coloring is necessarily light in tone, the flowers being carried out in white and palest tones of creamy yellow, green and shell-like pink. Sage greens, with a bit of brown, are used in the stem and leaves.

In embroidering the flower tints, first lay the straight and slightly curved stitches which form the centre cluster, and for this use the Japan Floss of M. Heminway & Sons in shade Nos. 0432, 432, 433 and 434. Springing from this cluster are the slender stems of the developed blossom heads in Nos. 428, 429, 429½ and 430 of green. The same shades with the additional green of No. 431 and brown Nos. 229 and 230 are used in working the heavy stems and also the leaves. The shades of brown are sparingly employed. Each little starlike group which forms the blossom, shows radiating single stitches of mingled white No. 688 and yellow No. 645, or white and green No. 0432. Dotted between these stitches are French Knots in pink shades Nos. 1655 and 1657. These little knots are somewhat irregularly placed between the straight stitches, the number somewhat depending upon the size and arrangement of the first laid stitches— from eight to ten knots will be sufficient in the various clusters. The darker pink knots of course appear on the shadow sides of flower groups, and the white on the lightest portions. The star stitches of these clusters extend over the small flower stems giving the full feathery appearance, which is so pretty in the natural flower, while the French Knots give variety to the surface, well suggesting the tiny blossom heads seen in nature. Single-strands are used throughout in working both flowers and foliage. Turkish Floss, white, No. 691 is suitable for the scallop and a line of couching composed of about seven strands of white caught with pale green is a pretty finish above the buttonholing.

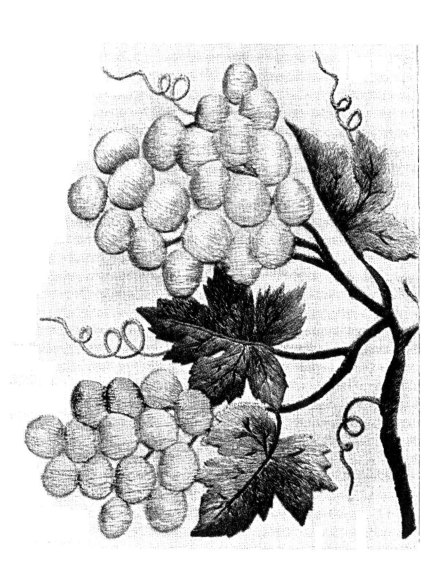

NO. 2900WT

Wheat Centerpiece.

See Color Plate No. 1.
Design No. 2900WT.   Sizes—
12, 18, 22 and 27 inches.

M. Heminway & Sons' Japan Floss. — Yellows — 361, 0409, 409, 409½, 0645, A645.   Greens —0432, 433, 433½, 434.

Turkish Floss.—White—688 or 691.

Description.—Pad the kernels with cotton and cover in Kensington stitch.   In either the golden tones of ripe or the sage greens of unripe grain this centre is extremely pleasing. Work from tip to base of each kernel and in entire head, afterward making the whisps which spread out at sides.   For yellow grain begin with 361, two strands at top kernel, gradually work succeeding rows darker, with shades 0409, 409½, etc.   Where shading is introduced in single kernels use one thread.   For green treatment, begin with correspondingly lightest green or white and work darker.   Do not make each head alike and let one side of some be in shadow and accordingly darker.   Use Turkish Floss, for buttonholing scallop, couching seven strands of yellow Turkish Floss 361 with single strand of green 312 above the white.

Grape Center.

Design No. 2930.
Size, 27 inch.

Use M. Heminway and Sons' Japan and Turkish Floss in executing this design.

JAPAN FLOSS.

Grapes.—Reds—490, 491, 492, 492½, 493.   Greens—310, 310½, 311, 0682.

Foliage and Stems.—Greens. —395, 396, 397, 398, 398½. Browns--228, 230, 230¾, 230E, 230D.

TURKISH FLOSS

Scallop.—White—691.
JAPAN FLOSS
Green—682.

Description.—Underlay   the

NO. 2930

grapes with cotton filling before embroidering in Kensington stitch. This padding should be at right angles to embroidery, and the Kensington stitch laid in straight stitches lengthwise of each grape. Color plate 15 gives a good disposition of colors for catawba shadings, while variety may be obtained by alternating clusters of green grapes with these. When green is used, the lighter shades given above should predominate, and whether the grapes be green or red, there must be a proper feeling of roundness in the entire cluster. Think of the light as coming from one definite direction. This simplifies and gives truth to the rendering and the result accordingly is far more pleasing to the eye.

Foliage.—Work the leaves either solid or in long and short, commencing with two strands, and shading with one. Blend in occasional touches of brown in the leaves. Give attention to the direction of stitches in the leaves, the proper slant for which is shown on the color plate. Use browns freely in the stems, which should be worked solid.

Scalloping is done in White Turkish Floss No. 691, and the tiny leaf spray in the small scallop is of 682 Green Japan Floss.

Wild Rose Key.

Materials.—M. Heminway & Sons' Japan Floss.

BLOSSOMS.

Pink	580.	Shade No.	1
	581.	" "	2
	0582.	" "	3
	582.	" "	4
	583.	" "	5
	584.	" "	6
	585.	" "	7
	586.	" "	8
	586½.	" "	9
	587.	" "	10

STAMENS.

| Yellow | 647. | Shade No. | 12 |
| | 648. | " " | 13 |

LEAVES AND STEMS.

Green	0428	—A.
	428	—B.
	429	—C.
	429½	—D.
	430	—E.
	431	—F.
	431½	—G.
Brown	...230	—H.
	230¾	—K.
	230E	—L.

THORNS.

Old Red . 529 —M.

M. HEMINWAY & SONS

WILD ROSE.........Color Plate No. 16

Reproduced from original models embroidered with
Permanent Oriental Dyes. Japan Floss

CENTER PIECE 2981A.

Sizes: 12, 18, 22 and 27 inches.

Wild Rose.

Design No. 2981A.

Color Plate No. 16

The great popularity of this dainty little flower almost causes a miscarriage of the justice, due to its sweet charm, so often do we see it poorly interpreted and executed— literally, without reference to its prettily modeled and undulating petals. If legend is to be accredited, our admiration is of long and hereditary standing, for 'tis said that it was Eve's kiss which caused the first wild rose to blush from white to pink. Centre No. 2981A shows a graceful arrangement of this pretty floral favorite, true to its poetic significance, which typifies simplicity.

The shading should vary in the different flowers, and no fixed lines should be followed, duplicating every shade and curve in roses or in petals. Location has much to do in the determination of lights and shadows, which should be carefully studied before the work is begun.

For the edge of upper petals of some flowers, use light pink or yellow, according to flowers selected. The same rules applying equally well to both colorings, and the two having a very refined and artistic effect, lying next to each other. For the pinks, use on outer edge 580 Japan Floss, two single strands drawn at one time from skein, the twist running down from eye of needle, to avoid roughing and wrong shading as well; tip three petals lightly with light green 395, single strands, shading down with 581, 0582 and 583. On outer edge of lower petals, reverse this shading by starting with darker pink 584, gradually shading lighter toward centre. A good effect is had by shading from side instead of upper edge of petals, some dark to light, and reversed. The finished petal should have an even, glossy appearance, and care must be taken not to draw or pucker the stitches, or overcrowd them. The turn over petals are some of lightest, others of darkest shades, the latter where lying most in shadow. Turn overs should be padded *before* and outlined *after* embroidering. Buds are pink 585 and 586. Some of the open, and also fallen petals, may be varied by using 581 for top and shading darker with 0582, 582 and 583, directly in centre of flower. For the round dot, around which the seeds are placed, use 483. This is worked solid in satin stitch, with underlying stitches in reverse direction for round effect. These centres are very important, as they give expression to the flower, and may render it "stiff" or graceful, according to the treatment received. The stamens and pollen are worked with 410 and 646, and should be placed irregularly around the centre dot of green. The stem stitch and French Knots make this familiar centre, the outer row of seeds, or knots being darker, and are first worked. A good effect **is** had by using a single strand each of yellow and brown together, or light green with either, for the knots, which should be firmly attached to surface.

Where the under side of rose shows, the shading deepens toward calyx, the upper portions of which are light, growing darker toward stem.

The leaves are commenced, like the flower petals, with two strands, using greens, 482 on tip, shaded with 481, lighter toward midrib, shading darker 482 and 483 toward stem, using one strand for all except outer edges of leaves. Vary the leaves by using lightest green on tip and old wood shades or burnt rose 235, 236 for old leaves and thorns. For other leaves, use 0428 to 431 and 235. also 236, for the russet tinge of leaves, which may begin on edges in some cases.

The stems shade from light to dark, according to location, being darkest where most in shadow, and are worked in irregular stem-stitch, with touches of 235 and 236. These shades are also used for the thorns, which are worked by taking stitch from inside of stem to tip of thorn, followed by others in same direction, and continuing for a short distance down the stem, and shading farther down with green.

The shell-edged scallop is buttonholed in 691 White Turkish Floss, with couching of color above, either pink 581 or green 0428. The larger plain edged divisions with scroll ends may be either white with colored couching, or pale green 0428.

NO. 2741

Trumpet Vine Centerpiece.

Design No. 2741.

Color Plate No. 9.

Size, 22 inches.

For this design, use Japan and Turkish Floss in the following colors:

TURKISH FLOSS
Scallop.—White—691.

JAPAN FLOSS
Pinks—0655, 655, 656, 657, 657½, 658, 659, 660, 661, 662. Greens—512, 513, 513½, 514, 515, 516. Yellow—363. Browns —229, 230¾.

The trumpet vine is a particularly effective centerpiece for a dining room with dark wood work such as Flemished or Weathered Oak.

Description.—B e f o r e embroidering, pad the outline of buds and the flared chalice of the flowers. For dark blossoms in profile use two strands of reds—662, 661 or 660 on the petal edge—into these blend 659, 658, 657½, 657, 656, 655, and finish with 0655 next the green of the calyx. The order may be reversed in light blossoms which may shade from 0655 at the chalice edge through the above mentioned shades, the flower tube ending with 660 or touches of 661.

M. HEMINWAY & SONS

TRUMPET VINE......Color Plate No. 9

Reproduced from original models embroidered with

Where a perspective of a flower is represented, showing thereby the opening into the trumpet, dark flowers are commenced with the same shades, working through 658 or 657½ into yellows 365 and 363. On this yellow are small French Knots of dark red. The stitchery must of course point in toward the center. The flower throat may show 657½ directly beneath the flare of the trumpet and from this run to deeper shades at its base. The same general directions, carried out with the paler shades, apply to light flowers which may also have touches of 363 yellow on their frilled edges. Buds may be likewise toned from light to dark or vice versa—beginning at the top and where the shading runs into palest pink, a few stitches of green 512 will be very pleasing. Use greens 512, 513, 513½, 514, 515, 516 and browns 229, 230¾ for leaves and stems combining several tints in one leaf. Direct the stitches from the tip and margin toward the midrib of each leaf and work this latter in a darker shade than elsewhere used in the leaf. A good feeling of light and shade is obtained if one side of a leaf is carried out in generally lighter tones than those used on the opposite side of the vein. Sparing touches of the browns mentioned will give variety. Ordinarily, thick stems should be of stronger color than the leaves they support. The scallop calls for white 691 Turkish Floss, and couching inside the scallop may be done with white or colors, according to individual fancy.

Daisies, White and Yellow With Clover.

Explanatory of Color Plate No. 3.

Shades required in M. Heminway & Sons' Japan Floss.

WHITE DAISIES.

BLOSSOM.	LEAVES AND STEMS.
White—691.	372.
Green—682.	372½.
Pinks—1655, 1657.	373.
Yellow—648, 650.	374.

YELLOW DAISY.

BLOSSOM.	
Yellows—645, 646	
647, 648	LEAVES AND STEMS.
650, 652	As above, or 512 line.
0410.	
Brown—230 G.	

CLOVER.

BLOSSOM.	LEAVES.
Pinks—330, 331, 333, 334, 335.	372 to 374 or
Green—311.	311 to 313.

WHITE DAISIES.

With two strands of 691 work tops of petals and work in single strand of pale green 682 at base. Occasionally use pinks 1655, 1657, either on outer edge or shaded into white. Centres of French knots in yellows 648 and 650 or slightly underlay a portion of centre nearest you, indicating thereby its height, and cover with satin stitch, filling in remainder with knots. Use two strands for stems and leaves and keep the latter serrated by working slightly beyond the outline over all serrations.

YELLOW DAISY.

For outer edges of lightest petals use two strands of 645 and work in single strands of 646 or 647 at centre. Darkest petals are worked in same manner with 650 and 652 and occasional single threads of 0410. Intermediate petals are worked with the other shades given in color list. Have a well defined feeling of light and shade with petals gradually changing from light to deep tones; do not scatter light petals hit or miss in shadow portiv. of blossom. Centres when seen full face are worked as described above. Profile shows centre to be quite thick and conical. Pad this, and cover with satin stitch, and crown with French knots. Leaves are worked as in marguerites.

CLOVERS.

Underlay entire blossom with filling cotton, with greatest height at base and through centre. Filling stitches are always laid at right angles to the embroidery. With long and short stitch and two strands of green 311 or white 690, cover this padding. Now thread 12 threads of pink, 330, in large crewel needle, and with stitch approximating ⅛ inch and nearly the same distance apart work across the blossom top with half the stitch on silk and half extending over on linen. Follow this with 331, 333, 334, 345 in succeeding rows across silk foundation, always taking end stitches over on linen. Flowers may also be shaded by having the high light 330 across top, and extending entirely down one side, the other shades worked in to bring the shadow portion on opposite side. The flower head should rest on top of its leaves, and accordingly the leaves are worked first. A more or less regularly defined crescent shaped high light is the characteristic marking of clover leaf. This always appears in the leaf centre near the top, with crescent ends pointing downward. White clovers may be worked as above, using 691 with pink of 330 line or 391, and touches of 393 when depicting the faded brown seen in nature.

The clover, we are told, is the symbol of industry and it would seem the bees must have bestowed upon her this honorary degree in recognition of her sweet ministerings to their busy days.

IMPORTANT.

To intelligently follow the embroidery lessons in this book don't fail to secure of dealers a sample card showing the silk itself in every shade made in all sizes of silk threads. See illustration on page 85.

M. HEMINWAY & SONS

WHITE and YELLOW DASIES and CLOVER
Color Plate No. 3

Reproduced from original models embroidered with
Permanent Oriental Dyes. Japan Floss

Daisy Center.

Design No. 2900D.

Sizes: 12, 18, 22 inches.

2900D.

Use *M. Heminway & Sons'* *Japan Floss* for floral decoration, and *Turkish Floss* for scallops.

Flowers and Foliage.—For shade numbers refer to reference table of page 39, and to article on page 40, for proper directions for working.

Scallop.—691 white Turkish, couching of green 370 if desired.

A pretty, naturalistic grouping of daisies is shown in centre No. 2900D, and no better arrangement can be found for this artless little flower. The daisy, or else the "Eye of Day" Chaucer calls it, and his many laudations of the floweret are but reiterations of the poetry of all ages. It has ever been, save with the farmer, a flower universally beloved, and many are its quaint titles in many languages. The French name "Marguerite" has a Greek origin meaning pearl, in accordance with its symbol of innocence. Prettier, however, is the Danish, meaning "a thousand joys," or the Welch, signifying "trembling star." The Scotch have the humblest, but who shall say the least loving, they call the flower "Bairnwort" because it is so dear to children, who recognize in it, according to one authority, the one flower they may ever pick unchided.

M. Heminway & Son's Francais Darning Silk.

A soft finish fast dye silk, prepared expressly for mending silk, wool, or cotton hosiery and underwear.

Articles darned with Français Silk are very durable and are not a discomfort to the wearer, because of the soft and pliable nature of silk material.

Sold at hosiery and fancy goods departments in Dry Goods Stores. Price, 60 cents per dozen.

Made in black, white, light blue, cardinal, garnet, navy, tan, écru, brown, lavender, pink, gold and gray, heliotrope, bronze, Balbriggan, emerald, nile myrtle, Alice blue.

Yellow Daisy or Black-Eyed Susan.

Centerpiece. Sizes: 12, 18, 22 and 27 inches.

Design No. 2981B.

Color Plate No. 3.

M. Heminway & Sons' Japan Floss for decoration and Turkish Floss for scallop.

Japan.— Yellow — 645, 646, 647, 648, 650, 652, 0410. Brown —230, 230½, 230G. Green— Line 370 or Line 512 shading dark to 515.

Turkish.—White—691.

Description.—No filling is required for the petals of this flower which are worked solid with 2 strands on outer edges and shaded in with one. For

2981B.

light flower use 645 on tips of lightest petals, *i. e.,* those nearest you. Shade with 646, 647, 648 having the color deepest around the brown centre. 645 as the highest light must be very sparingly used. Generally speaking 647 will serve to tip the petals, and darkest flowers show 652 and 0410 around the centre. Where the under portions of petals show as in half open buds, these are lighter than the upper surface. Keep the flowers of large cluster in centerpiece darker at base of group, and shade lighter. Remember that strong contrasts immediately attract the eye, so these must not occur in unimportant flowers or portions of flowers. Use Brown 230 G for centres and refer to description of white and yellow daisies under color plate for the disposition of stitchery. Leaves are worked in usual manner with either the 512 or 370 line working darker from tip to base. Brown 230 and 230½ may be introduced for dead leaves. The buttonhole scallop is of Turkish Floss, white 691 and a couching of either yellow or green may be placed above this.

IMPORTANT.

To intelligently follow the embroidery lessons in this book don't fail to secure of dealers a sample card showing the silk itself in every shade made in all sizes of silk threads. See illustration on page 85.

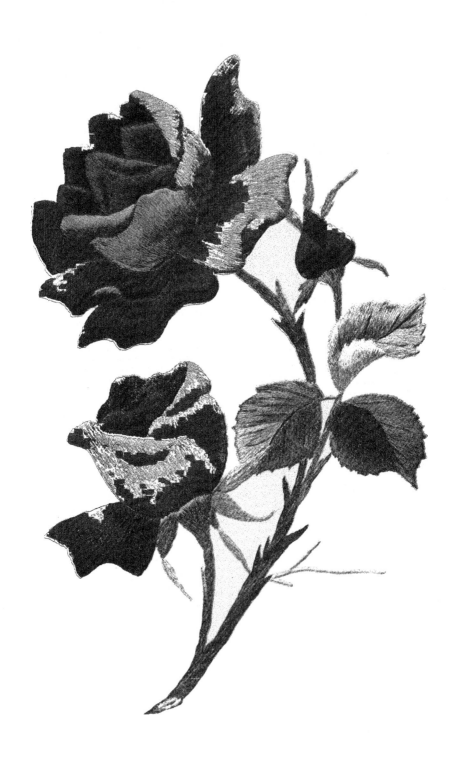

2980D.

Clover Centerpiece.

Design No. 2980D.

Color Plate No. 3.

Sizes: 12, 18, 22 and 27 inches.

Use M. Heminway & Sons' *Japan Floss* for decoration, and *Turkish* for scallop.

Japan.—Blossoms.—Green— 310, 310½, 311. White—688. Pink—330, 331, 332, 333, 334, 335. Brown—391, 393. Leaves —372 to 374.

Turkish.—White—691. Green —310½.

Description.—After carefully reading the method for working clovers given under color plate article on page 40, no further instruction should be necessary. Use pinks from 330 through to 333 for lightest flowers. 334 and 335 must appear in darker ones. Additional shades will not always be necessary in producing darker appearing flowers, and a fairly deep flower may be the result of colors given for the lightest one, if the deep shade in the latter is the one most freely used. For white clovers use the shades enumerated above. Give variety in the leaves, always carrying out the crescent like marking in a lighter tone than the rest of the leaf. Do not use padding save to indicate turnovers, then cover these with single silk strand of lighter tone than the rest of leaf. Outline the edge where turnovers rest upon the underlying portion, do not outline edge where they roll over from the foundation.

The large connecting scallop buttonhole in white 688 Turkish, and small sections outlying these, buttonhole in green 310½ Turkish.

Rose Decoration.

See Color Plate No. 4.

We are ever at a loss to offer due tribute to perfection, and, whether we would express ourselves in words or pictures, must ever feel inadequate. Accordingly, the needlewoman will find herself confronted by some difficulties when first she undertakes the embroidering of roses, but happily the florist's art gives us roses all the year and a little careful study of a natural flower will solve many of her problems. In no other flower is there such constantly changing direction of stitches. Petals will curve inward and wrap themselves around the heart of the rose, or roll outward, all in the same flower. A feeling of roundness must always be preserved throughout the flower, and no petal should seem flat, or all sense of contour will be lost. Modelling, or producing the appearance of a changing surface in embroidery is the result of carefully directed stitches, so at no time must one depend upon color to correct faults of needle craft. The truth of this can be proved by good examples of Chinese or Japanese embroidery, many of which although rendered entirely in one shade, give a fine feeling of form due to their intelligent needle guiding. As no two flowers ever grow exactly alike, neither should any two be worked in identically the same manner, that is to say no two upon the

NO. 2979. SIZES: 12, 18, 22 AND 27 INCHES.

same piece of needlework. Avoid monotony in color and stitch directing; repetition invariably produces flatness. Let there be a slight contrast between the several roses in the same group. Do not try to apply coloring which is not in accordance with the variety of roses pictured. This applies most especially to American beauty roses, the formation of which is much heavier than that of other roses. Never use the American beauty shades in roses which are of other types, or you will be working to produce an erroneous effect. Remember that the sunlight seems to act in a contrary manner upon green leaves and flower petals. Greens increase in intensity, other colors fade with the sun, so that a rose past its prime is paler than an opening bud while young leaves are many shades lighter than those fully developed. All colors merge into some tone of brown as they wear old, and the woody structure of large stems often requires shadings of brown or red. The youngest shoots and leaves also show pretty touches of brownish reds and it is well to observe these variations, selecting silks, however, which will not be too strongly opposed to other colorings in the design. It must be remembered that we should not always reproduce things just as seen in nature, for even that brave dame is not beyond the evil influences of environment and "there is an art which does mend nature."

M. HEMINWAY & SONS

TEA ROSE...........Color Plate No. 4

Reproduced from original models embroidered with
Permanent Oriental Dyes. Japan Floss

Tea Rose Centerpiece.

Design No. 2940R.

See Color Plate 4. Compare Color Plate 14.

Japan Floss.—Green—Line 480. Brown—229, 230¾, 230D. Yellow—A645, 411, 647, 650. Red—529. Lilac—590. Tea Rose—280, 281, 330, 331, 332, 580, 341, 342, 340, 343, 333, 480.
Turkish Floss.—White—691.

A section of a Tea Rose Centerpiece is shown at color plate No. 4, and the entire design pictured on this page shows a beautiful piece of decoration containing only roses of facile interpretation.

2940R.

Description.—Lightly underlay the outer edges of flower petals and pad the turnover portions to a slightly greater height. Use two strands for margins and turnovers, shading in with single strand. For top petal touching leaf cluster use 280, 281 with single scattered threads of 331 and for turnover use 330. In next to top petal use 341, 342 and a touch of 330 with 480 at base. Use 330 also in this turnover. The same order of shading is used in other petals, the turnover of forward upturned petal is 580. The deeper tones of 331 and 332 are used in lower petals. All petals shade from pink at margin to a touch of green at their base. In the bud use two strands of 331 and 330 for outside of deeper petal and 330, 580 and A645 on the lighter portion. Make turnover of 580. Excepting 331 and 332 all above mentioned shades are used in lingering petal of the fallen rose. Yellows 411 and 650 are used in stamens and anthers, the latter composed of French knots. Stems worked in line 480 with occasional red 529. Direct stitches of leaves from tip and margins toward the mid rib, use line 480 and shade in 229 and 230¾, 230D, also 590 for old leaf colorings. Vein with red or brown in these and use red in thorns. Couch 7 strands of 691 above the scallop with a single strand of yellow 647.

N. B.—This rose is quite similar in shape and coloring to the beautiful Irish Rose of Killarney.

Conventional Wild
Rose Center

For Fish Net Inser-
tion.

Sizes: 12, 18 and 22
inches.

The same style can
be obtained in con-
ventional poppy, No.
2986/2, three sizes on
white linen.

First baste the fish
net on the under side
and work the button-
hole stitch with silk
through the linen
and net after which
cut out the linen as
shown in illustration.

Turkish Floss is
used exclusively—
style of coloring can
vary—natural flower
tints not strictly nec-
essary.

NO. 2986/1. QUARTER SECTION.

Suggestions for combinations are:

Flowers—Pink	Leaves—Poppy Green
" —Nile	" —Dark Sea Foam
" —Maize	" —Lily Green

For the centers of the pink and Nile flowers, use old gold Nos. 409½, 0410.
For the centers of the Maize flowers use browns Nos. 0410, 410, 411. No. 683
Nile is an appropriate shade to use in button-hole stitch on the border sections.
Other designs arranged for fish net that can be obtained of dealers in M. Hem-
inway & Sons silks are:

No. 2986/2 Poppy.
No. 2985/1 Conventional.
No. 2986/3 Conventional.
No. 2985/6 Conventional.

N. B.—*Send six two-cent stamps* to the publishers of this book (see title
page) at Watertown, Conn., for their book of thirty pages, size 8x11 inches,
containing eighty illustrations of Eyelet Embroidery and Hardanger work with
silk.

2981D.

California Pepper.

Design No. 2981D.

Sizes: 12, 18, 22 and 27 inches.

Use Japan and Turkish Floss of M. Heminway & Sons for decorations and scalloping of the edge.

The California pepper is always a favorite in needlework, and design 2981D makes a charming table decoration. In general, the coloring seen in embroidered California pepper is too deep, and we give in this article the proper nature tints.

Description.—The berries are embroidered in satin stitch, and leaves and stems in Kensington stitch. In coloring they range from palest green to a bright glowing pink, and delightful combination is afforded by the changing tones, where in a single cluster, the green berries gradually ripen to pink. For green berries use a single strand of 0682 running in 310½ and 311. Semi-ripe coloring calls for 0682, 310½ greens and 404 pink, in others 636 pink may be added to the above shades. All pink berries may be worked in 404, 636, 637 and in a few, run in for deepest pink 638.

Leaves and stems are worked in the 310 line, but only a sparing use of the deepest 313 is recommended, just enough to give accent, but not so much as to render the greens sombre and uninteresting. Browns 300. 301 and 302 also work in to good advantage in the stems and old leaves.

For the scallop use Turkish white 691. A couching of pink and green may be placed at top of larger divisions finishing with scroll ends. For this use 8 strands, 3 of Turkish 404 and 5 of green 310½ and fasten them down with a single strand of green 313.

N. B.—We have no retail department or facilities for filling orders from private parties, but will cheerfullypforward to nearest dealers any retail orders sent us.

Prices at which white pure linen stamped doylies and centers are sold by storekeepers are: 12-inch, 15c.; 18-inch, 30c.; 22-inch, 50c.; 25-inch, 60c.; 27-inch, 75c.

M. HEMINWAY & SONS SILK CO.,
Watertown, Conn.

"Lazydazy" Decoration.

Design No. 2965c/2.

Centerpiece. Sizes: 12, 18 and 22 inches.

Color Plate No. 11.

A charmingly decorative center-piece is pictured in the accompanying "Lazydazy" design. It combines individuality and novelty in effect, brought about through simple stitchery.

The dainty, feathery clusters of the blossom are among the most familiar of the late summer flowers and their very facile rendering in embroidery is a happy conception As the illustration indicates, the flowers are carried out in bird's eye stitch which is merely a loop held in place by a short stitch

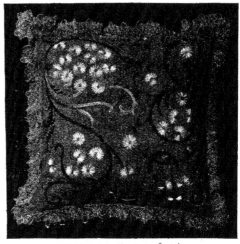

PILLOW DESIGN 2965P/2.

at the end. By means of this stitch, the many petals are readily produced and small clusters of French knots are used to form the centre. Two strands of M. Heminway & Sons' Japan Floss or one strand of Turkish Floss give the desired effect for petals. The delicate fernlike foliage requires fine, even feather stitch, and one strand of Japan Floss must be used here in order that the original fragile structure of the leaves be fitly represented.

Any woman having a good color sense may give herself free rein in this design which is equally pleasing whether executed in different tones of one color or in combination of tints. The latter effect was chosen for the center-piece model illustrated, the result being a charming harmony of lilac tints together with tones of pink and blue, and soft dull olive greens.

Description.—For the lilac tints, shade numbers 590, 591, 592, 593 of M. Heminway & Sons' Japan Floss will prove most effective, blending easily with pink cluster carried out in Nos. 540, 541, 542, or 543. Suitable tints of blue are found in numbers 628, 629, 630 and the appropriate tones of green are

2965c/2

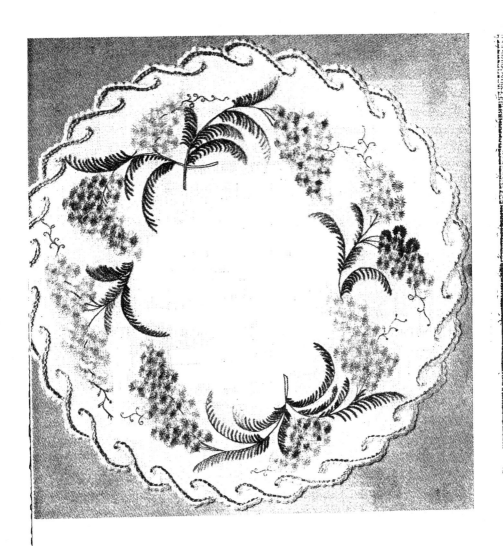

M. HEMINWAY & SONS

"LAZYDAZY"......Color Plate No. 11

Reproduced from original models embroidered with
Permanent Oriental Dyes. Japan Floss

Nos. 428, to 431 and 512 to 514 with an occasional blending of brown No. 230¾. The yellow centres are worked with Nos. 647 and 649. The nature tints of lilac, with white, are no less pleasing than the conventional colorings of blue or pink given above. Deep shades in all cases, must be used sparingly, for the color scheme should be soft to be pleasing and in harmony with the airy structure of the natural flower. For the scallop 691 Turkish Floss should be employed while a deft touch of color is given by couching seven strands of No. 683 pale green with one strand of the color predominating in the flowers.

A single color in its various tones may be used in the flower cluster throughout the design. For the pillow, Turkish Floss is best suited. Dealers can furnish the design stamped on homespun linen—backs of same material. Darker tones of color should be used to bring out the best effect. Rich reds and deep yellows are appropriated for the clusters on the homespun back ground.

Fish Decoration.

Shades used in Color Plate No. 13.

M. Heminway & Sons' Japan and Turkish Floss.

Japan Floss.—Gray—395, 396, 397, 398, 399, 1196, 1198, 1200, 1202. Purple—589, 1475, 1477. Pink—232, 0235, 0238, 581, 582, 0582, 1655. Green—434, 0682, 682. Serpent—520, 522, 523½, 671, 673. Brown—226, 227 229, 230½, 230D, 230F, 409½. White—691, 341.

Turkish Floss.—White—691.

A section of centre 2880 is the subject of color plate 13. It presents an admirable rendering of fish, gliding in among seaweed and white coral. The complete design has two smaller fishes with coral and weed, and the finished piece is unusually effective and unique.

The plate well illustrates the color and stitchery of the fish, the shade numbers are given below. The Kensington stitch may be begun back of the gills working on to the slender joining of the tail. The tail may be worked from the ragged edge inward. Pad the outline and division lines of gills, and work from these forward to the mouth. Along the back and beneath the dorsal fin, use gray green 399, shade through 398, 397, 396 and 395 and then into grays 1196, 1198 and 1200. The green of the back is dashed with blue 673 and occasional stitches of 230 maize. As greens approach the grays the brown dashes change to 230 and 226 and pale blue dashes of 671 are seen over the 395 and gray tones.

The head is lighter in general tone, the edges of the gills are 395, a few dashes of 671 are worked over the blending in of 396 and 397. Back of and inside the mouth is 398. The mouth is worked in 606 and a bit of 607 salmon. Use 409½ for the eye, the stitches of which are slanted, following the circular shape—the pupil is a French Knot of 690 black.

With two (2) strands of 399 work the serrated edge of tail and fins. Shade lighter toward the body using, in the tail, the entire 395 line. Blue single thread stitches on fins and tail are 693.

Scale markings give the finishing touch to the fish. These consist of the arrow point stitch which is described among the fancy stitches in the front of this manual. Use 673 for scales on the green, and 1202 when working over the gray.

In the shell seen below the fish, the ridges of the convolutions are rʳ with chain stitch of cotton, also the top which rolls back. Begin with strands of pink 582 at the pointed tip, use 0582 for second division, 581 for third. The fourth is begun with 589 lavender and a single strand of 1475 shades into this. 0682 green commences the next, while the above given lavenders blend into this where the coral crosses over the shell. In the last and largest division the colors are placed in the following order: 691 white, 0682, 682 green, 581 pink, 1475 lavender and 0582 pink, render the rolled edge. The inside of the shell calls for 1655, 581, 582, while the rolled edge is carried out with satin stitch in 691.

The coral is perhaps the most interesting part of this decoration, so wonderfully realistic is its rendering, and yet it is very easily accomplished. First underlaid with cotton, it is afterwards covered with satin stitch, the stitches placed at an angle, as in heavy stem-stitch. It is the clever introduction of French Knots on top of all this which gives the true coral appearance. The knots vary slightly from the ordinary, each one having a little stem, as it were. That is, the needle is put through to the right side, the thread wound around it, and it is then inserted about an ⅛ of an inch from the point where it first appeared. Use white 691, cream 341 for the lightest portions of the satin stitch, shading into 1196 and 1198 for darker portions, and 1200 and 1202 where one branch falls behind another. The knot stitches correspond to the foundation in shade number, save that 341 is always knotted with white.

Delicate tracery of sea weed is carried out in purplish reds, 232, 0235, 0238, and water lines are outlined in 520, 522, 523½ serpent greens.

The scallop is long and short buttonholing of 691 White Turkish Floss, and Japan Floss in green and pink, shade 682 and 1655, are worked in irregularly in the order given, the pink extending well up from the edge and often partly hiding the water lines.

Two smaller fishes are worked in gray and brown respectively, and in the following shades. Gray fish 1196 through to 1202, 691, 0682 lines in fins, and scales 230F, mouth 607, eye 409½ with dot of 690. The brown fish has head and gills of 226, 229 and 230½. Along the back is the darkest coloring which shades light toward the tail. Use 230D and 230F and gradually work lighter, using the shades given for the head. Gray shades in the under part of the fish, 1196 and 1200. Scale markings are of 434 green, which also is dashed in the fins worked in 230½ and 230D. Occasional bits of green weed require 0432 and 434 green. The center shown here is ᵗe similar to design No. and the description given is applicable for both.

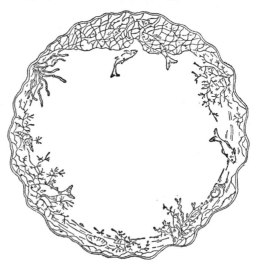

DESIGN NO. 2750—25 INCH

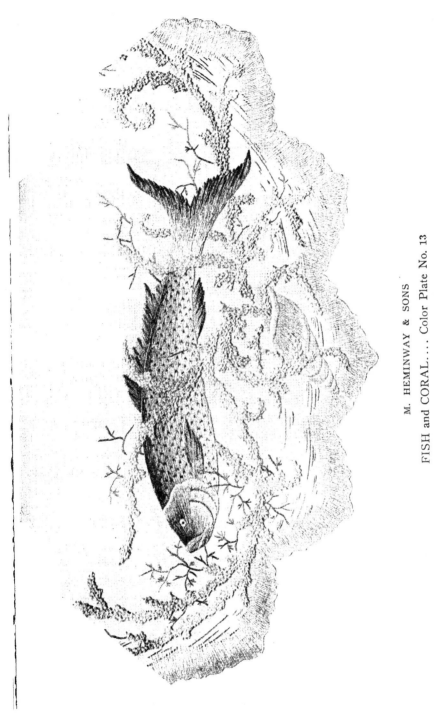

M. HEMINWAY & SONS

FISH and CORAL.... Color Plate No. 13

Reproduced from original models embroidered with
Permanent Oriental Dyes.   Japan Floss

Syrian Centerpiece.

Design No. 852c. Size, 25 inch.

SYRIAN DESIGN. NO. 852C. EMBROIDERED.

Syrian embroidery is a new form of needlework which is especially adaptable to old conventional patterns. Centre 852C, which is worked on coarse
homespun linen, illustrates this novelty. The method of working is extremely
simple. The design scrolls are divided into sections, and the embroidery consists in working in satin stitch and then outlining on three sides of each section.
The effect is that of overlapping scales, which is the characteristic of Syrian
design. In the long scroll pattern illustrated, these scales seem to spring one out
of the other, like the growth of some varieties of cactus.

Underlay the work with cotton, and the use of colored filling is recommended, infinite varieties of shading being obtainable. The satin stitches are
laid to follow the growth of the scroll. Use Turkish Floss of M. Heminway &
Sons for Syrian work in numbers 525, 526, 526½, 528 and 530. Reds make an
attractive coloring with the lightest shade used on the two top and bottom
scrolls. The second pair from top are in 526. 527 makes the first curve as
the branching spreads to the sides, and 530 completes the branch. Above is a .
group of two scroll curves in 526½ and 530 makes the last section of this branch
ing. The outlining for each section is done with the same silk as its satin s

filling. Use 528 for scalloping and couch or outline above this with a lighter shade. The 290 line in old blues, the 370 line of greens, or the 0408 line of yellows are also recommended.

SYRIAN DESIGN. NO. 852C. SIZE 25 INCH.

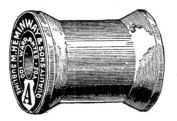
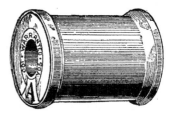

Pansy Decoration.

See Color Plate No. 17.

DESIGN NO. 2921P.   SIZE: 22 INCHES.

Comparatively few specimens of this "vigorous and various" flower are shown in color plates, as there seems to be no limit to the innumerable variety, the possibilities of color and combination of this offspring of violet parentage. Indeed there are few tints and tones not called upon to contribute to its generous "makeup," the effect of which bears so closely at times upon an almost human-featured face, that the appeal to the imagination is irresistible.

It is difficult to realize that, in its original state, the pansy was a tiny "tri-color" of one variety, plain in garb and sombre tint, a veritable little quakeress among her gayer sisters. But we are told that in the early part of last century, it was unknown to cultivation and general recognition, growing wild as a common weed, its beauty "born to blush unseen;" but its "sweetness" was not destined for the "desert air." Its evolvement was due to the fancy of an English girl, who found a plant by accident, and who, pleased with its appearance, planted and replanted its seed, and gave them all such careful attention that she was very soon rewarded with a succession of blooms of constantly increasing design and variety, which improvement continues to the present time. The evolution of to-day, like pansies, "is for thoughts."

While the best models for the embroideries may be taken from the growing plant, for every tone of whose flowers there is a match in M. Heminway & Sons' Japan Floss, some of the varieties in the illustrations here shown may be selected for further guidance, and being copied from nature, are true in color and union, while innocent of exaggeration.

A very effective one is that in dull pinks, and it is worked in Japan Floss, numbers 231 to 0236.

Another, in shades of 231, is combined with Yellow beginning with 360, shading as deeply as 367.

The very rich purples, 1477 to 1489, are used alone for some. A different tone of same color, 589 to 595, for still another, and a variation of this is 556 to 561. Some of these are purple alone, while some have markings in yellows and pale straw color.

The effect of rich crimson velvet is brought out in some of the flowers by using 527, 528 and 529, lined with black or golden-brown, while this latter color, No. a408, and yellows 0645 to 653 are artistically combined.

A white pansy is made by working the surface in white, 689, beginning with two strands, and using next a single strand of white, which will make a decided shade, and shading toward centre with Green, 0682. The three lower petals or "face" being lined with 1485 purple.

Pale Pink Pansy.—341, 344, 345, 413; lines in face, 528.

White and Purple.—691, 682, 683, 1475 to 1481; lines in face, 1485.

Yellow.—0645, 646 to 649; lines in face, 411 or 529 or 1487.

Purple.—1475 to 1487, or 590 to 594; lines in face, 646 or 1491 or 651. Dull Purples—270 to 275; lines in face, 646.

Golden Brown.—0408 to 410; lines in face, 415¾ or 1489.

Purple and Pink.—1475 to 1487, and 341 to 346; lines in face, 1489.

A good effect is obtained by using two strands of 1475 as margin of face, shading with Yellow a645, using a single strand and through these shades to 648, making the lines in face 1485, the two top petals Yellow, a645 to 648, or Purple, 1475 to 1481. For the centre use 650, Yellow, and on either side a stitch of Green 370 or 0428.

These combinations could be indefinitely continued, but the most satisfactory way, which is nearest truth, is to use the freshly cut pansy from the plant. Having matched the various shades with the Japan Floss (as before suggested) to the natural flower with the latter before one, it would be difficult to make an error in its reproduction, unless one is "color blind," in which case embroidery of any kind should be out of the question.

Different tones of Green which make a very good effect, are employed for leaves, stems and calyxes, and these two tones are blended in a single leaf or separately worked as preferred—481 to 486 are soft shades and harmonize with the wood color of basket and the flowers above, while 240 to 243 give a touch of brightness and life to the foliage. The curved stems when thrown against the background are worked light, the calyxes light at tips, shading darker toward stems; the latter having any length are worked light through the centre, shading darker on sides. This preserves their raised and rounded form and the same rule will be found to apply to most of the stems in embroidery, position, of course modifying them.

The rounded effect must also be studied in all curved petals, and with this end in view one should commence with two strands of Japan Floss in extreme edge of petal (both strands removed at once from skein, their twist running *down from* needle), and following the shape of petals place stitches so that they will fall in what would be the natural grain or line, not pointing sharply to centre, as in case of many leaves; into this first row, work next shade, using a single strand and so continue to the centre or eye, or as the pansy wears so human an expression, one might say the "nose," which is of Dark Yellow with a stroke of Pale Green or White on either side. The three lower petals are called the "face," and it is there that the "expression" properly placed gives it character and individuality, and where the "lines" should evenly, regularly and lightly lie.

M. HEMINWAY & SONS

PANSIES............ Color Plate No. 17

Reproduced from original models embroidered with

2940P.

Pansy Center.

Design No. 2940P. Sizes: 12, 18, 22 inches.

Color Plate No. 17.

M. Heminway & Sons' Japan Floss for floral decorations and Turkish Floss for scallops.

Japan Floss.—Purple — 349 350, 351, 352, 354, 355, 356, 1477 and 1485. Yellow—0645, 646, 648, 651, 653, A408. Green —370, 372, 373, 374, 375.

Turkish Floss.—White 691.

Description.—Anyone of the other combinations given with the color plate may be added to this scheme of yellow and purple, suggested by the color line. We recognize the mad wisdom of Ophelia saying, "There is pansies, that's for thoughts" when we begin to embroider them, for they do require thought and discrimination if their rendering is to be successful.

Use 691 Turkish Floss for scallops. Above large portions ending in scrolls, couch 7 strands of combined 1477 purple and A408 yellow, with single strand of 1485 purple.

Rooster Decoration.

Shades Required.

M. Heminway & Sons' Japan Floss.—Old Reds— 526, 526½, 527, 528, 529, 530. Yellows—0408, 408½, 0409, 409, 409½, 0410, 411, 412. Black—690. Brown —624. Greens—433, 433½, 434½, 434½, 435½. Gray —1200. White—688.

Either as a picture, pillow, or as the base of a tray, the splendid cock forms an excellent example for needle painting. Since the cocktail tray has insinuated itself in many a household, the housewife who is looking for pretty novel conceits,

will be pleased to see this one which she can readily carry out at the point of her needle.

A deep bevelled picture moulding will serve as a tray edge, and when the linen is tightly stretched beneath glass and firmly fitted with a light wood back, a very satisfactory tray results to which a practical finishing touch is given, by attaching to each end light metal handles.

In embroidering birds of any sort, close attention must be given to the stamping, that the formation of the feathers be not lost. One must feel that each feather overlaps the one beneath, so there must be careful adherence to outlines. Let us begin with the comb which, must first be padded with chain stitch of cotton along the top. For the color use M. Heminway & Sons' Japan Floss. Select 526½ for the high lights along the top of the comb points—shade 527 into these below and to the right, which is the shadow side. Into this 530 runs, with a few split strand stitches of 690 black, close to the head. The wattles also must be padded along their lower edge. Turn the work, and proceed from padded edge to the head with the same order and shades as given for the comb. The breast is darkest beneath the wattles shading from 530 to 528, 527, 526 and 526½ at the high light placed in the most prominent part of the breast. The same shades then work back to the dark feathers of the legs. The direction of stitching is simple and easily discernible in the illustration. Dark brown 624 is worked in among the stitches of 530 deep maroon in the leg feathers, and each one of these is outlined with black 690 to define it. The feathers of the breast are marked by means of small crescent curved lines of couching, a single strand couched with the same shade, and corresponding with the shade of Kensington stitch which it overlays. Wings and tail feathers are glossy green. In the wing, the stitch curves as indicated by the pattern, and each long feather is shaded from upper to lower edge with green 435½, 434½, 433½, and an outline of 690 is placed between each. The tail feathers show a central shaft toward which the stitches slant, and for these, to the greens used in the wings, should be added 433, also occasional split stitches of the golden yellows mentioned later. One's judgment will suggest keeping tips, and most prominent feathers light, and shading dark close to the body. Use black or dark green outline for the central shaft, according to the tone of each feather.

For the bill use 0408, 408½ and 409. A line of 409½ separates the two portions of the bill, which should be padded on its edges. For head and back the shades are 0408, 408½, 409½, 409, 0410, 411, 412. The feathers are lightest just beneath the comb at the curve of the neck and where they fall over the top of the wings. The long pendant feathers at the back call for deeper shadings and defining tones of still darker tones. Irregular stitches placed over the embroidery of the neck will suggest the idea of overlapping feathers. Split stitches of 409½ should run over the red of the comb, and a shadow of 0410 above the eye and back of the bill throws them both into prominence. The legs and toes are embroidered lengthwise with 0409 and the scales are marked with outlines or fine couching of 412. A stitch or so of 690 black and 1200 gray forms the claws. The eye setting has a ring of red stitches 527 pointing into an outline of black. An outline of 688 is placed next, then white again next to the black pupil.

Tiger's Head Decoration.

Explanatory of Color Plate No. 10,

Embroidery of regal splendor is presented in the accompanying Tiger's Head which is adaptable to an elaborate Princeton pillow, or fire screen, should one

M. HEMINWAY & SONS

TIGER............Color Plate No. 10

Reproduced from original models embroidered with
Permanent Oriental Dyes, Japan Floss and
Turkish Floss

wish to put it to a practical as well as ornamental use, which it does not obtain when simply framed as a picture. The gorgeousness of color demands a fitting background, and a sumptuous and wholly appropriate mounting is afforded by heavy black silk or satin.

The illustration should be well studied before commencing one's piece of embroidery, for the direction of the stitches is of prime importance and this must not be forgotten if successful results are desired. More latitude may be taken in the placing of colors than in the slant of stitches, a fact which ofttimes escapes the mind. The Turkish and Japan Flosses of M. Heminway & Sons are used throughout in this piece of needle painting, Turkish Floss for the most part, softened by single threads of Japan.

The forehead is a good place to commence the stitches, slanting back from this point gradually change in direction between the ear and eye to curve down and backward near the ear, and downward round the eye to the throat. These general directions are indicated by the stamping. More delicate modeling is required about the muzzle. Directly between the eyes, the stitches follow the slant of the nose, while they change in direction lower down, so as to curve across above the nose, and sweep down around the open, snarling mouth, depicting the wrinkled jowl. In working in the various shades the needle must be slanted through in a gliding manner, never inserted directly up and down. The triangular shape of the nose dictates the slant of its stitches, which run straight up from the point above the teeth, and outward over each nostril. The stitches at the side of the nose follow it in direction and are modified slowly so as to run in with those of the cheek. In the eyes, the yellow iris is worked round the black pupils and a high light is carried out with a straight backward slanting stitch. Above the eye, the stitches curve upward giving the bushy effect of the eyebrow. The directions for teeth, beard and whiskers are plainly discernible in the color plate. An occasional glance at the pet cat may prove helpful in embroidering the tiger, for the two are close of kin and fur grows alike whether in the western world or the jungles of India. If one has a good picture of a tiger's head, this also will be of great benefit, and with attention, patience and careful following of the directions, the problem need not prove so difficult as to discourage the careful worker. Reference to the tinted head, displayed on linen pillow top No. 2500/1, will be of great service, even when working on a dark or satin background. Sold by dealers in M. Heminway & Sons silks.

Color Description.—The lay of the stitches being well in mind, as before mentioned, begin at the forehead, the slight arch of black Japan Floss No. 690 giving a definite starting point. The stripes across the top of the head shade from black to bright golden brown and back to black, Nos. 548, 547, 411 and 0410 and occasional stitches of No. 409 being required to give the proper gradations. Light gray and yellow appear with brown and black on top of the ears, 0409 and 0408 being the yellow tints, while 1202 gray is softened by single threads of white Japan Floss No. 688. The ear tips are brown, say 548, and black appears here as well as in the deep shadows under the ear. All of the above mentioned browns and yellows, together with black and white are worked into the hair as it curves down under the ears and back to the neck which ends with dark brown No. 549½. A dark stripe of black and brown extends from behind the ear standing in sharp contrast with a light stripe which precedes it, and which brings into use all the lightest tones of maize and yellow, with white. Extending from the forehead down above the nose, the bright, strong, yellow and browns prevail, while softer tones again take precedence at each side of the nostril. On the nose 0408 shades into tan 226 and then to 690 white. A bit of red 659 may be worked in above the black of the nostril. The reds of the tongue are 658, 660 and 662 worked in 690 black in the shadow under the teeth, which latter are worked with 1202 gray and 1196 also black and 0408 yellow. The beard shows the same shades of gray with white 230D brown, and light touch of No. 0408 yellow. The bushy hair above the eyes calls for 0408 and 688 white, 690 black and single stitches of 1202 gray. The eye itself shades from light to deep yellow while the pupil is black with high light of white. Eyebrows and whiskers are the finishing touches and these are done in white underlined with black.

Too much cannot be said regarding the single thread stitches of Japan Floss which must be used throughout this design, working them over the heavier Turkish Floss. The same shades will be required in Japan as in the Turkish Floss and these soften and blend in the shades, greatly adding to the general effect.

Horse's Head.

Design No. 2500/3.

2500/3

M. Heminway & Sons' Japan Floss. —Browns—547, 548, 549, 622, 623, 303. Tans—229, 230½, 230¾, 230E, 230F, 230D. Grays—1196, 1198, 1200, 1202. White—691. Black—690.

No fitter picture can be found for a needle picture than the fine sorrel horse's head which is illustrated. Such a picture is well worthy of the embroideress' best efforts and she will find this needle painting extremely interesting. The horse, his coat, glossy from good grooming is readily produced in silk embroidery and the full color line of M. Heminway & Sons' Japan Floss gives one perfect scope in shading. This attractive piece may be obtained, stamped and tinted from the dealers. Several methods might be applied in developing this study, each one with equal success, and she who feels herself competent to undertake so ambitious a piece may prefer to proceed after her own inclination, still for the benefit of those less confident, a description of a workable method may prove helpful.

To work from the top downward is the general rule for all embroidery and of course this applies here. Each stitch, however, must run from down upwards, the needle gliding in among the first made stitches; never insert the needle directly up and down, for unless the silk is made to shade in among the first stitches, proper shading is impossible.

Description.—With two strands of M. Heminway and Sons' Japan Floss 623, begin the tip of the ear and work down along the outline about ½-inch, directing the stitch slightly toward the inside of the ear. Brown 622 follows this along the side of the ear nearest to one, and 547 may be used on the opposite side. The inside of the ear should be worked in 548, 549. White and black in single thread must be sparsely worked over these to give proper depth of shadow. Here the stitches slant, following the directions of the ear toward the head. The same silks and general shading apply to both ears, the edges being kept lighter than the inner and outer portions.

From the ear, next work down the neck giving constant thought to the slant of the stitches, for the sleek coat must never appear to be rubbed the wrong way. 622, with the stitch directed downward, starts back of the ear and following the direction of the throat lash, 623 is worked into this. Once away from the outlines, single strands should be used and one shade worked gradually into the next without any perceptible line. The stitches of the neck must of course follow it in contour and extend well up under the mane. Into 623 work in 547 and 548 and extend this down into and around the high light of 622 which gleams on the front of the neck. Black 690 must be worked over the brown beneath the mane and also directed under the throat lash. The space between the ears is mainly covered with the forelock, but 622 should be at the side of the right ear and, as in the case of the mane, carried well under. Working down the face, the stitches beneath the head band spread out to right and left toward each eye. 622, 623, 547, 548, 549 and 230¾ browns, together with 690 black are required in this portion, the black and light tan 230¾ coming least into play.

Browns shade to tans and change to grays in the nose, and here more than ordinary attention must be given to the lay of the stitches. 229 and 230 are the additional tans required to shade into the sorrel tints, a small patch of these appearing just above the nostril and at the right side of the animal's white nose marking, which will be referred to later. Shades of gray 1198, 1200 and 1202 together with black 690 work out the muzzle and nostril edge. The grays are worked around the nostril rim 1202, with scatterings of black shading to 1200 and 1198 around the mouth which is defined by a line of black. The turn of the nostril is worked in 1200, the stitch here running in toward the opening as in the working of any oval opening. Within the nostril, use 548 worked over with 690.

The eyes next demand attention. The folds of the eyelids are executed with stitches running lengthwise, of course following the corner. For these, use tans 230½ and 230¾, 229 with darker tints of 547 and 548 defining the creases. Beneath the eye, 690 black is worked over into the browns of the face referred to above. The eye is worked in 548 and 690 with an outline of 548 and 230¾. The lashes and high light with 1196, 229 and 622. The white patch of the nose we leave until the last. Just between the eyes is the pretty star marking with the stitches radiating from the centre and continuing the length of the nose. 1196, with touches of 1198 form the main part of this marking which gives both the character and high light to the whole picture. Single threads of the palest tan 229 are sparingly worked in along the edges of this, and in one or two places are little spots where sorrel speckles the white in a very natural fashion.

The mane and forelock require good handling of tan 230F, 230E, 230D, 230¾, 229 and occasional bits of 622, 548 and 549. Let the stitches curve gracefully over the arch of the neck and show a slight undulation back of the ears. Use the darkest shades most sparingly, merely occasional threads of 548 and 549, keeping the forelock in the three lightest shadess of tan. The bridle should be worked in 690 black with an inner line of 303 and buckles of 1202. The stitches of course, follow the curves of the various strappings and are worked toward the centre for buckles and rings. This design tinted on Tan Ticking can be obtained at stores where M. Heminway and Sons' Silks are sold. Price with back material, 60c.

Daisy Centerpiece.

NO. 799C.

Materials—M. Heminway & Sons White Mount Mellick Silk, size G, White Linen Satin Damask.

German Mercerized Coronation Cord, size 15.

Description—The stems are outlined in silk; the leaves worked in plain satin stitch; the centers of the daisies in French knots; the petals are formed by appliqueing—two kernels of cord to each one—and the cord is couched on the double lines that form the border of the design.

The method of attaching the cord is to first make a hole in the linen (at the base of the flower) with a stiletto (see page 16), or point of scissors, draw the cord through the hole and fasten down on the wrong side with the same silk used in the other parts of the design.

The space between the two lines of cord on the border is filled in with fancy feather stitches.

This design is also well suited for the use of Turkish Floss—and may be preferred by some, because of its flossy smoothness, and great brilliancy, though Mount Mellick Silk, being quite a firm twisted silk, is more appropriate, if durability is to be considered.

This white center piece is a universal favorite, worked as described.

N. B.—We have no retail department or facilities for filling orders from private parties, but will cheerfully forward to nearest dealers any retail orders sent us.

Prices at which white pure linen stamped doylies and centers are sold by storekeepers are: 12-inch, 15c.; 18-inch, 30c.; 22-inch, 50c.; 25-inch. 60c.;

M. HEMINWAY & SONS SILK CO.,

Watertown, Conn.

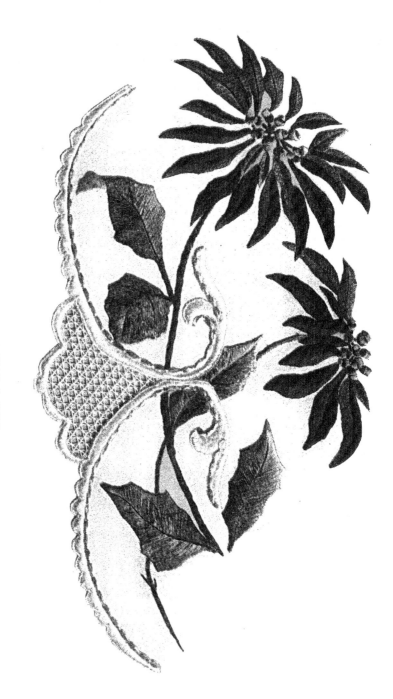

M. HEMINWAY & SONS

POINSETTIA......... Color Plate No. 12

Reproduced from original models embroidered with

Permanent Oriental Dyes. Japan Floss

NO. 2980F.

Poinsettia Decoration.

Description of Color Plate No. 12 and Centerpiece No. 2980F.

Sizes: 12, 18, 22 and 27 inches.

Materials—M. Heminway & Sons' Oriental Dyes Japan and Turkish Floss.

For the Flowers—Japan Floss—Reds.—6, 8½, 10, 10½, 013, 017, 019.

Leaves—J a p a n F l o s s— Greens—371, 372, 372½, 373, 374, 375. Old leaves—230, 230D.

Center of flowers—373, 374, 650, 654.

Scallop—Turkish Floss— White 691, Green 310½, Pink 581.

Work the top petals of the California Poinsettia in the three lighter red shades—using the darker ones for the lower petals; use more of 10½ and 013 as these two colors predominate in that flower—the flaming reds. The centers of the flowers are in green 373 and 374. For the bulb at the top use yellow 650, also a little of 654. The leaves are in the sage green 371 to 375, shading as in the ordinary leaf, using a little of the brown shades 230 and 230D in with the green for the old leaves.

The scallops in this center are worked with 691 white Turkish Floss. The couching above the scallops is in green 310 Turkish, using light strands fastened down with one strand of white 691 Turkish Floss.

In each section above the small scallops white fish net is inserted. Fancy stitches can be used in this space instead of the net if desired.

Poppy Decoration.

See Color Plate No. 18.

To effectively work the Poppy or any other flower of like proportions having open petals, it is best to commence at top of petal, gradually shading through the deeper tones to desired effect, being careful to work the tones irregularly into each other with uneven stitches so that they will blend with no line of demarkation. The order of color is reversed where opposite effects are to be attained, and much depends upon position of flowers upon the article to be worked and that of the different petals in relation to each other.

To work this design as illustrated, commencing at top of straight petals, work with two strands of silk drawn at same time from skein which has previously been cut through either end. These strands will be short, but as there is no difficulty in renewing the thread in this style of embroidery it will be found that the work will be smoother. See that the twist runs to lower end of strand—that inserted in the work—and have this direction uniformly maintained. This may soon be easily distinguished by passing the silk between the forefinger and thumb and a little practice will enable one to readily discover the direction of twist. If this rule is observed the shading will be much more uniform and the work much smoother, as there will be less liability for the silk to roughen in passing through the fabric to be embroidered. Do not use smaller needle than No. 8 for double thread and No. 9 for single thread, that the silk may have full play through the slender eye lying flat upon work when distributed and not be crowded or twisted upon itself.

The Red Poppy in color plate is worked with shades 655 to 661, the light and medium shades sparingly, as a reference to color plate will suggest, and the lightest for the "high lights" as indicated.

Should it be desired to have the work heavy, as is appropriate in flowers of this dimension, begin with three threads, instead of two, of same shade; shading into this consecutively with two and one strand. The turn-over sections are worked "solid" or in "satin stitch," being first padded or dashed back and forth, most of the thread lying upon the outside and in a direction opposite to that of the "satin" stitches. This "turn-over" portion is sharply outlined on either edge, not blending with anything, but resting naturally *upon* and *outside* of rest of petal.

Make pollen and stamens black, 690, and the bulb of 371 and 373.

The small poppy is worked in Japan Floss. Nos. A655 to 656, and the color plate will best serve to illustrate its fine and delicate shading.

The leaves are worked in shades 370 to 374, using two strands on outer edge. of leaf, shading toward centre with one strand.

The fuzzy effect of stem is made by taking on each side of stem when finished, at irregular intervals, with one strand, short stitches in 370 and 371 at right angles to stem. Buds in 370, 372, 373, light at tip, shading dark to stem. The flower part of buds darker than body of poppies to which they are attached.

The white poppy is worked almost entirely in No. 691, shading toward base and when shadows are naturally cast into Pale Nile, 0682, 682, 683. One petal should be touched with 405, 406 and another with 404, 0405.

M. HEMINWAY & SONS

POPPY..............Color Plate No. 18

Reproduced from original models embroidered with
Permanent Oriental Dyes. Japan Floss

2940PY.

red and 682 green, fastened with 374 green.

Holly Center.

Design No. 2981E.   Sizes:
12, 18, 22 and 27 inches.

Use Japan Floss of M.
Heminway & Sons for floral
decoration and Turkish Floss
for scalloping this design.

Japan Floss.—Red—8, 8½,
10, 10½, 011, 013, 015. Green
—370, 372½, 373, 374, 375.
Brown—230,   230¾,   230E.
Black—690.

Turkish Floss.—White—691.
Green 683.

Description.—The most effective holly is dark with crisp
high lights, position and size
of leaves largely determining
their coloring—underlying ones
being deepest, smallest ones
brightest, and those nearest
one, ˉlightest in tone. For

Poppy Center.

Design No. 2940PY, Sizes: 12,
18, 22 inches.

See Color Plate No. 18.

Use Japan Floss of M.
Heminway & Sons for floral
decorations, and Turkish Floss
for scalloping.
Japan Floss—Red—2 through
to 015. Yellow—645, 647, 650.
Black—690.   Green—0428 to
431½ and 682, 374.   Browns
—228, 230½, 230E.
Turkish—Green—683.
The article "Poppy Decoration" following color plate No.
18, makes description of this
centre unnecessary the disposition of color being so well
exemplified.
Scallop.—Use 683 Turkish
for scallop, and inside this a
couching line of blended 0408

2981E.

small bright leaf begin with 2 strands of 372½. Extend a stitch at the point to make these sharply defined. Shade 373 and 374 into this with single strands, directing the Kensington stitches toward the mid rib from each side. Vein with 375 for contrast. Under sides of leaves are always light—372, 370 with occasional bits of brown 230 near the serrated edges. Use browns 230, 230¾ and 230 E, together with 375, 374 and 373 greens for old and withering leaves —and the veining in these may be light. Berries are worked in satin stitch from stem to pit. Use 8 and 8½ for lightest, 10, 10½ and 011 for the majority and 013 and 015 in the darkest. Make a French knot of black 690 in representing the tip, or miscalled seed.

For large scallop ending in curved lines use 691 white and 683 green.

Turkish Floss is very pretty for the remaining portions. Couch above **the** scallop if desired.

California Poppy Decoration.

Descriptive of Color Plate No. 7.

Embroidered with Japan Floss.

Flowers.—Yellows—360, 361, 362, 363, 366, 367, 0409, 409½, 409, 654, 654¾. Dull Reds—235, 236.

Foliage.—Greens—371, 372, 373, 374, 375, 241, 241½, 242. Browns—300, 303, 304.

Description.—Underlay edges, petals and turnover portions with chain stitch of cotton before embroidering in Kensington stitch. Commence with two strands of silk, well covering the outlines, then shade in with single thread. The central full bloom flower of the color plate utilizes the following shades. The petal to the left is edged with 361, into which is shaded 362, followed by 363, single stitches of 409½ spread out like rays where the petals join the calyx. The opposite petal is begun with 360, then 361, 362, 363 with a few stitches of 0409. The lower petal shows darker coloring as it is begun with 409½, shades into 409, then into 362. The turnover is worked in 363. The top petal is lightest of all, 360 extending well into the petal before it blends into 361, 362, 363, and 0409. The turnover is of 409. Ray like stitches of 409-409½ extend out from beneath the pistil of green, and similar stitches of dull red 235 and 236 are worked over and among these. Pistil of green is tipped with 372 and finished with 373.

The next largest flower being less opened is of darker coloring. The central rear petal is begun with 409½ and a very few stitches of 0409 at its left hand edge. 409 works immediately into these and is brightened with 366 then 367 and a few final stitches of 654¾. 409, 366 and 367 are used in order named in the tiny petal at the left. The upper right hand petal is begun with 0409 with 409½ and 409 following. The forward petals are light, the larger one running from 0409 into 409½, and finishing with 409. Turnover of 361. The small petal begins with 361 and finishes with 367. The same shades with exception of 654¾ appear in the full right-hand bud, while the dark shades are again prominent in the small bud low down on the decoration. One bud shows the yellow just bursting and lifting up its odd little protecting cap of green which so quaintly suggests a candle snuffer over a yellow flame.

373 and 374 greens are used for the calyx, with touches of 303 and 304 browns. The foliage, light and feathery in structure, is consistently so in color also. The soft tones of 371 and 372 and 241 are the predominating ones, while a more sparing use is made of 241½ and 242. 373 and 374 are also used,

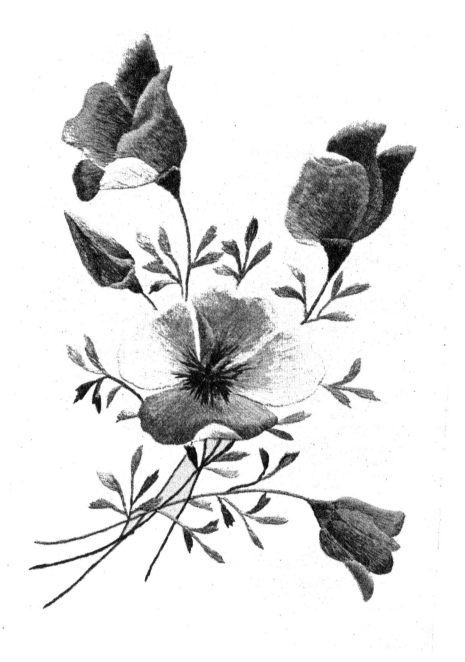

M. HEMINWAY & SONS

CALIF

the latter serving to give accent. Stems are mainly 373 and 374. 302 and 303 browns give an appreciable variety in some of the tiny leaves. The green cap on the bud before mentioned is worked with 372, 373 and 374 with a few stitches of 375 on the shadow side.

NO. 2980 E.

California Poppy Center.

Design No. 2980E.

Sizes: 12, 18, 22, 27 inches.

The proper colors for this design are enumerated in the article concerning the color plate, and the flower is so simple as to require but little supplementary remark. Although it be but repetitions to write it, still we must emphasize the need of variety in shading, for variety is all the more necessary where the decoration is composed of flowers of a single color, as in this center.

The scallop may be elaborated by lines of couching above the larger portions. Turkish Floss 691 should be used for the button-holing, and couching of green 371. Seven strands fastened, with 374 green will be attractive, the small divisions may be buttonholed entirely with 372, with feather stitch lines of 371 springing above them. The yellow of the blossoms being such a positive color, it is advisable to introduce only greens in the scalloping in addition to the white.

Publisher's Special Notice.

This Treatise on Embroidery is not a regular catalogue of all designs supplied to dealers, the entire line being much more extensive. It is the purpose of the publishers to be able to fill wholesale orders for designs shown herein for some time to come, but to keep pace with the requirements of the art stores for new things the arrangement of flower sprays and borders will be changed.

We have no retail department or facilities for filling orders from private parties, but will cheerfully forward to nearest dealers any retail orders sent us.

Prices at which white pure linen stamped doylies and centers are sold by storekeepers are as follows: 12-inch, 15c.; 18-inch, 30c.; 22-inch, 50c.; 25-inch, 60c.; 27-inch, 75c.

M. HEMINWAY & SONS SILK CO.,

New York. Philadelphia. Chicago. San Francisco.

Carnation Center.

Design No. 2980A.   Sizes:
12, 18, 22, 27 inches.

Use M. Heminway & Sons'
Japan and Turkish Floss for
this decoration.

In addition to the colors
given with Carnation Color
Plate No. 20, the following
shades for white and yellow
and red flaked blossoms will
be found attractive. Combinations of the various colored
flowers will be charming if
judiciously arranged, but one
must remember that while in
Nature's landscape embroidery
the most startling juxtaposi-
tions are encountered, the wise
needlewoman will limit her
color scale to more subdued
and recognized harmonies.

2980A.

For white blossoms the following may be employed No. 691, 340, 341, 342, or
a645, o645, 645 cream or yellow, o682 and 682 green and 580 and 581 pink.

It will be well to use the yellow tones in the shading, not relying upon green
alone which makes the flower too cold in tone.

Yellow flowers, flecked with red, are always decorative and require the following shades: A645, 645, 646, 648, 649, 650, 651 652 with 10 and o11 for the
irregular splashes. The 370 line of green with 228 and 230½ brown will be
required for the foliage.

For Pink Carnations see reference table on page 92.

For the scallop use Turkish Floss 691 white for the large divisions. Couch
green 310½ above this if desired. The small divisions may be carried out in
green 310½ with feather stitching in color No. 2 pink or green on the lines above.

Carnation Decoration.

Descriptive of Color Plate No. 20.

The Carnation, "the flower of Love," comes to us with many a classic asso-
ciation, and though it has submitted to a changeful category of names, we may
be sure, that like its fair sovereign the rose, it, too, by "any other name, would
smell as sweet." Owing to its adaptable structure it was used by the ancients
for garlands which crowned their heroes, and some authorities claim the popular
name is a corruption of "coronation," while others as stoutly aver that the name
results from its carnation coloring. The spicy fragrance for a time led to its
being classed with the gilly-flower, and it was an important factor in mulled
wines, while the ancient pharmasepœia listed it among cures for fever.

M. HEMINWAY & SONS

CARNATION........Color Plate No. 20

Reproduced from original models embroidered with
Permanent Oriental Dyes. Japan Floss

The variety of its coloring greatly adds to the popularity of the flower, and also makes it a most interesting study for the embroiderers. The most usual tones of deep pink and red are represented in the color plate, while various other colorings are suggested in connection with the carnation centre elsewhere mentioned. The petals farthest from one should present the deepest coloring, which gradually works lighter as petals come nearer the eye. Take for instance the largest flower on the color plate in illustration. The rear petals are worked in long and short Kensington, beginning at the highest with 6, 8 and 8½ of M. Heminway & Sons' Japan Floss. Dashes of 10½ are seen in the two lowest rear petals. Double strands of silk are always employed to cover the outline, while shading is worked in with single thread. Turnovers and fore-ground petals have an underlay of cotton. The palest petal shows 2 and 4. Nos. 6 and 8 are run in the slightly deeper ones flanking it. Turnovers are of No. 2. The next deeper flower utilizes the above shades with 013 and 015 additional. In the small dark flower the shades show a sparing use of 8½ and 10½, 013, 015 and 019 complete the list.

For foliage the colors are selected from the 730 line of green with touches of 230E and 227 brown. The lower parts of the long green calyx are padded, and are lightest at the upper points, 372 and 373 or 373 and 374 are used for these. Greens are deepest just between these points, 374 or 375 being required while the coloring works lighter where the calyx ends. 370 is used in the pale leaves together with above mentioned browns. The lay of the stitches is so simple in carnations that inspection of the color plate is adequate instruction.

Nasturtium Decoration.

See Color Plate 19.

Design No. 2940N.   Sizes: 12, 18, 22 inches.

M. Heminway & Sons' Oriental Dyes, Japan and Turkish Floss.

Shades for flowers and leaves.—See description table illustration, following page.

Before starting to embroider this flower, it would be well to first put in a little filling of white embroidery or darning cotton, on the outer edge of all the petals, just enough to raise the edge above the centre, to give a "cup" effect to the flower. A chain stitch is a simple and easy method of filling the outer edge of petals. If darning cotton is used, take the cotton that can be split, using two strands.

Work the flower solid, in the long and short stitch, using one strand of Japan Floss.

If no filling is used, work with two strands of Japan Floss, on the outer edge of petal, shading with one strand. Some prefer this way to using the filling.

For a Light Yellow Nasturtium, start with Yellow, No. 360, Japan Floss, on the outer edge of one or two petals, shading with No. 361 and 363. The lower petals make darker, using No. 363 for outer edge, shading with Nos. 364 and 365. The rays in flowers can be made of Orange, No. 654, or Red, 529. In heart of flower, use Brown, No. 549, in French knots. In this flower the calyx is Yellow, 650 and 367.

To vary the Yellow flowers, use Red 526½ and 527 for outer edge, shading with Yellow, 363, 364, 365 and 366. For rays, use Red, 527, in one flower, and 529 in another. In the calyx the Red, 527, and Yellow, 650 and 652, are appropriate.

In a Red Nasturtium, the shades 526½, 527, 528 and 529,

NASTURTIUM DESIGN, NO. 2940N.

Japan Floss, are effective with Yellow, 650 and 365, for rays, making calyx of Red, 526½ and 527, with Yellow, 653, at the tip. Another Red blossom can be made by using the Red shades, 526, 526½, 527, 528 and 529, not only for the petals, but for the rays and calyx.

The leaves are worked solidly in long and short stitch, using lightest shade of Green, No. 311 for the outer edge, shading darker until No. 312½ is in the lower centre part of leaf, veining with Light Green, No. 432, 311 or next shade lighter 310½.

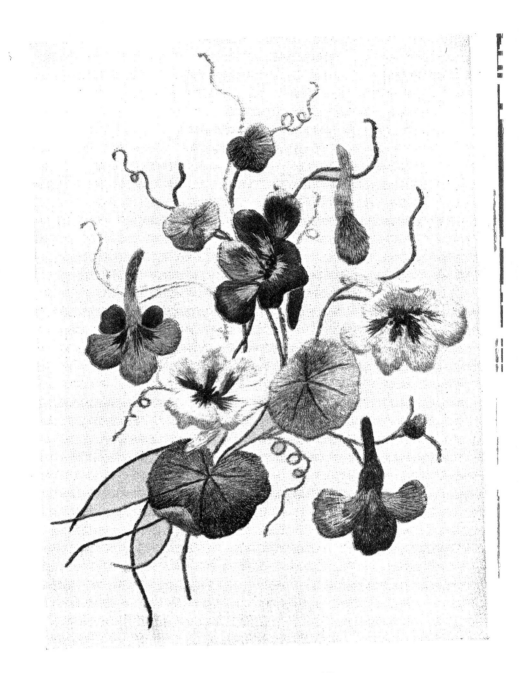

M. HEMINWAY & SONS

In other leaves use No. 312 and 312½ for outer edge of leaf having the lightest shade, 311 for centre, veining with 312½.

Never use filling cotton for leaves, except for the turned-over ones. Those should be filled well to distinguish them from the leaf. Work the outer edge of leaf with two strands of Japan Floss, shading with one strand. The turned-over leaves use one strand of Japan Floss to cover the filling cotton. The lightest shade of Green is generally used for leaves that turn over.

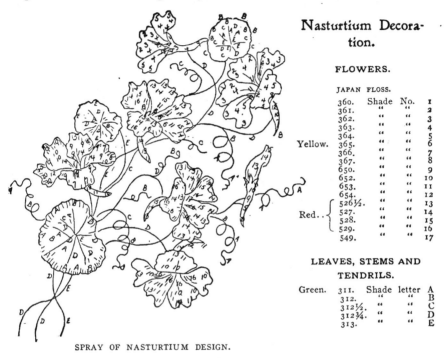

Nasturtium Decoration.

FLOWERS.

JAPAN FLOSS.

Yellow.	360.	Shade No.	1
	361.	" "	2
	362.	" "	3
	363.	" "	4
	364.	" "	5
	365.	" "	6
	366.	" "	7
	367.	" "	8
	650.	" "	9
	652.	" "	10
	653.	" "	11
	654.	" "	12
Red..	526½.	" "	13
	527.	" "	14
	528.	" "	15
	529.	" "	16
	549.	" "	17

LEAVES, STEMS AND TENDRILS.

Green.	311.	Shade letter	A
	312.	" "	B
	312½.	" "	C
	312¾.	" "	D
	313.	" "	E

SPRAY OF NASTURTIUM DESIGN.

"HANDY" HOLDER FOR JAPAN FLOSS.

A practical convenience for keeping skein silk in perfect order.

When covered with linen—embroidered with pretty design it makes a handsome gift.

Sold by dealers at 5c.

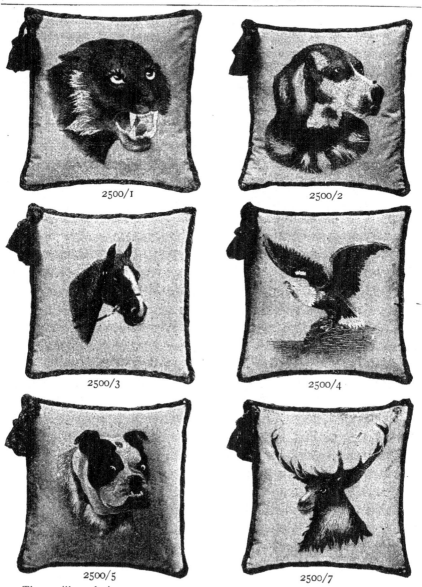

2500/1

2500/2

2500/3

2500/4

2500/5

2500/7

These pillow designs tinted on tan ticking are sold by dealers in M. Heminway & Sons' silks.　These models worked in Turkish Floss.

College Pillows and Designs.

By Edgar P. Redfield

College pillows grouped artistically about the "den" and cosy corner, or thrown here and there on the window-seat or in the boudoir, form a pleasing decoration and add a charm to the interior. In every well appointed country home or city appartment one sees the cosy corner literally filled with pillows of every description, while all through the house and out on the veranda they are much in evidence. In fact, as is often said, one cannot have too many pillows, for aside from the artistic effect produced, they have a certain charm of refinement and air of comfort and repose which seems to invite one to nestle among them and while away an hour or more, if it be "my lady" with her favorite magazine, or if a gentleman with his evening paper and after-dinner cigar.

In selecting pillows it is an easy matter to go to the shops and purchase the finished article or choose a pattern stamped ready for embroidering with the materials to finish; the only thought being "Is the design striking or pretty? Do the colors blend artistically or is the pattern odd and attractive?"

In selecting a *college* pillow, however, one must be more critical and first of all see that the colors are correct. Each college or school has its standard color, as the rich blue of Yale, the crimson of Harvard, the rose and gray of Vassar, the blue and red of "Pennsy," the yellow and white of Bryn Mawr, the orange and black of Princeton and so on. Correct colors therefore is the first essential in selecting the college pillow and must be strictly adhered to. These colors can be obtained in the various grades of satins, as well as in the better grades of art linens which are dyed especially for this purpose and woven in the proper pillow width.

Next in order comes the design. Every university and college or school of prominence has its own particular emblem or seal, which is used in ornamenting its stationery, invitations, programs, etc., and through the cunning of the jeweler's art is reproduced in rings, charms and pins of gold and silver. These designs used in so many ways and which become endeared to the hearts of the students and friends of the various centers of learning, lend themselves especially to the decorative feature or motif of the college pillow. They carry with them a certain amount of dignity, are official, and appeal directly to the sentiment of every one interested in the particular college or school they represent. Other effective designs are the simple block letters, forming the college name and running diagonally across the face of the pillow, and the large initial directly in the center. These, while severely plain, are very striking.

The irregular style of lettering, as shown in the illustration on the following page, is a pleasing departure from the many styles of script and fancy lettering, and is particularly adapted to the formation of long names, as Pennsylvania, and University of New York. The letters are graceful and can be arranged so as to fill in well, giving the pillow a decidedly artistic appearance.

A very pretty design, but which can be used only in connection with a name of four letters, is the large four leaf clover as illustrated, a letter being in each leaf. Many original designs are especially good. Often a young lady of artistic temperament and skilled in embroidery has ideas of her own regarding the pattern she desires to embroider, and produces at once a design both striking and novel. As an example of this may be described an original conception in the way of a design brought out by a lady having friends in both Yale and Harvard and who was very much interested in the football games between the

two universities. She took as her motif the two sculptured figures by J. Massey Rhind above the portico of Grant's Tomb on Riverside Drive, New York City. These figures flank a panel on which are enscribed the words "Let us have peace." One figure she embroidered in Yale blue, the other in the Harvard crimson, each holding a football and wearing the regulation uniform so familiar to everyone attending the annual games. The words "Let us have peace" were embroidered on the panel between them. The design as adapted to a pillow was decidedly good and very effective.

In embroidering the college pillow be careful to select the right shade of silk, where a color is to be used, always bearing in mind that in embroidering they work up a little lighter. Letters should be worked solid to produce a good effect, while emblematic devices and figures can be embroidered in outline or couched if preferred. Where there is a combination of two colors representing the college standard, as in the case of Princeton orange and black, Pennsylvania red and blue, or Vassar rose and gray, it is optional which way they are embroidered. Take Pennsylvania for example, the ground work or fabric of the pillow can be of blue with the seal or lettering embroidered in red, or vice versa. The front of the pillow also can be of one color and the back of the other.

Where there is only one color represented, as in Yale, Harvard and Columbia, the pillow itself should represent that color while the embroidery should be in white. There are a few exceptions to this rule, notably Harvard which is often embroidered in black. One sees occasionally the white satin pillow with the seal or lettering brought out in the college color which, though very pretty to look at, is so easily soiled as to be of no practical value. In embroidering, the work can be done more evenly and better by using any one of the many styles of embroidery hoops or frames to be had in the shops. After the work is finished, the pillow should be dampened and pressed on the *back,* having the front or face on soft material such as a flannel blanket and is then ready for finishing, either with cord and tassel or ruffle. Ruffles are strikingly handsome, especially on satin pillows, but the cord and tassel is more in vogue and makes a very neat finish. The usual position for the tassels is the upper right hand corner of the pillow.

For the filling, where one does not consider the expense, a pure down is undoubtedly the best, but cheaper filling such as silk floss is very satisfactory. *Never use cotton,* as it is hard, coarse, lumpy and very undesirable. A very pretty finished pillow lately brought out is made of a fine quality of felt with the seal or letters cut out and appliqued on with Turkish Floss, while the finer work, devices, figures, etc., are reproduced in India or colored inks. These pillows are finished with cord or by the use of a simple narrow ribbon, the front and back are held together, making a very neat finish.

Sometime ago, a gentlemen, himself a college graduate, conceived the idea or fad as one may call it of having a college room in his beautiful Colorado home. The writer had the pleasure of assisting him in the selection and making up of the pillows. A number of designs were submitted to him including college seals together with the costs of arms of West Point and Annapolis, and several special designs from which he selected in all some twenty-five or thirty. These were all embroidered entirely by hand on satin and art linens and finished with elegant double ruffles and silk cords and tassels, the whole forming a very attractive and artistic ensemble and delighting the eye of anyone fortunate enough to have the entree to his palatial home.

A list of some of the prominent universities and colleges, giving their colors, will be found on pages 96 and 97.

Information as to source of supply for pillow tops and backs in correct colors for any college will be furnished gratis by the publishers of this book.

Wallachian Embroidery.

When a form of embroidery is developed from already familiar, as well as simple stitchery, it paves its way clearly to popularity and success. Wallachian embroidery is a ready adaptation of an old and well known stitch, thus producing an entirely novel effect. Although the button hole stitch is the basis of this new work, the decorative effects produced by its characteristic designs, often suggests the more elaborate stitches of Chinese embroidery.

It is from the peasant workers that we generally obtain our needlework suggestions and women of Wallachia are the ones who have individualized this form of buttonholing. A centerpiece in Wallachian, pictured as a frontispiece, is an excellent example of this form of embroidery, showing both the simplicity of workmanship, and quaintness of design, together with a charming scheme of harmonious coloring. Details

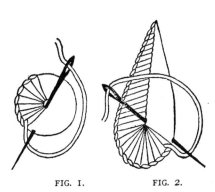

FIG. I.   FIG. 2.

DETAIL OF WALLACHIAN EMBROIDERY.

of the work shown at Figs. 1 and 2 prove the method of procedure to be plain
buttonhole. The units of all Wallachian designs are variations of two forms, each

with a predetermined
principle regulating
its method of working.
The two basic forms are
either variations of
floral and scroll mo-
tives, or of disc shapes.
In the first series there
is invariably a central
rib, and all the button-
hole stitches point to-
ward and end at this
line. In the units based
on circular forms, the
stitches all point to and
end at the centre like
wheel spokes. As the
many strands all end-
ing in the one place
make a small hole, a
good effect is produced
by first running this
centre dot around and
having opened the space
with a stiletto, allow
the button hole stitches
to finish through the
hole, thus making an
eyelet. Chain, cable or
outline stitch are suit-
able for stems or single
lines.

NO. 01970-5

COLLAR AND CUFFS IN WALLACHIAN EMBROIDERY. SEE FIG. I.

*Collar, neck measure, 24 inches, 4½ inches; cuffs, 3¾
inches wide.*

The buttonholing may be either raised or flat, depending upon the silk employed. The model for the frontispiece executed in Turkish Floss manu-
factured by M. Heminway & Sons shows the raised buttonhole, that is to say,
that which is slightly padded on the cord edge of the stitch. This raising may
be done with loose darning cotton and the edge either run or followed with
a chain stitch. The soft greens which appear in the illustration, are shade
numbers 239, 241, 241½ and 242 of Turkish Floss, while 691 white is also required to give the high lights in the shading. A simple and dainty scallop is
worked in shade number 239 which gives an appropriate and unobtrusive finish.
Of the three discs above the large lobe of this scallop, the central one is
worked in the same shade as the scallop, while those to right and left are
carried out in No. 241. The upright leaf spray is toned from No. 691 white
at top to 242 green at the base, while the flower form with the leaves and
stem shows the gradations produced by all four shades of green first mentioned.

Manifold color schemes may be evolved from the vast numbers of shades
available in the Turkish Floss. Delft colorings in shade numbers 290, 291,
292 and 293 are cool and charming with blue and white china. Decorative

tones of yellow are found in numbers 408½, 409, 410 and 411, while the old gold gleams of No. 599, 601 and 603 are particularly beautiful when combined with an ecru or natural linen background. This design is attractive when worked entirely in white.

The twisted Silk of M. Heminway & Sons is also effectively employed for Wallachian embroidery, either in colors or in white, and at Fig. 3 is pictured a detail of design 2960/2 elaborated with fancy stitches and worked in Mount Mellick white size G. A row of Gordian knot stitches appears above the buttonholing of the scallop edge, while the other portions of the design, excepting the stems, are edged with French knots, placed at intervals of a quarter inch or less. This same treatment in colors is very pleasing should one prefer it to the severer forms of an unornamented outline. A detail of Gordian knot stitch is given in the first part of this manual and will be found a very useful stitch, both effective and speedily executed.

FIG. 3. NO. 2960/2.

The above designs, as well as numerous other patterns are obtainable in a doylie size of 12 inches, also in centerpieces measuring 18, 22 and 27 inches. An entire luncheon set would not be an arduous undertaking in Wallachian work as it progresses rapidly, and the finished pieces are substantial both in fact and appearance, more than repaying by their durability the time given to the working.

Wallachian embroidery adapts itself admirably to many other articles beside those for table decoration. For all sorts of accessories, as well as for dresses it bids fair to rival the popularity of eyelet work, as it is applicable to all sorts of fabrics. For linen or pongee gowns it is most desirable both in colors and white, and waist and skirt may both be embroidered, or a simple model may be selected and

NO. 1970/6.

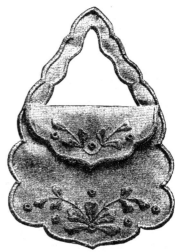

NO. 229/2.   NO. 207D.

trimmed with the very pretty revers and cuffs which are here illustrated. With stylish stock and belt of Wallachian, a gown of linen will be given decided *caché*. A Wallachian Chatelaine of linen can be had to match the belt, and this while adding much to the costume in daintiness will also bring its equivalent in usefulness. Lingerie hats are now a recognized necessity in the summer wardrobe, and will be made in Wallachian to complete embroidered cos-

NO. 2976/3.

BABY CAP. NO. 217/2.

tumes, or worn independently with any tub frock. For the little folks, caps and bibs are to be slightly ornamented with this newest embroidery, and the use of Turkish Floss is recommended for these in order that the results be firm and yet dainty in appearance.

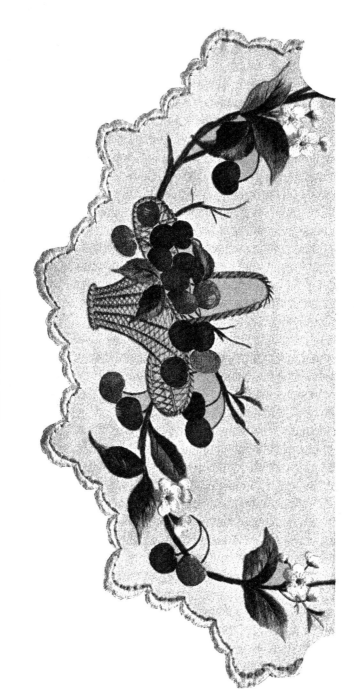

M. HEMINWAY & SONS

CHERRIES.........Color Plate No. 2

Reproduced from original models embroidered with

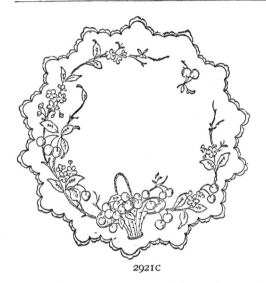

2921C

Basket of Cherries.

Design No. 2921C.

Color Plate No. 2

Centerpiece—Size, 22 inch

M. Heminway & Sons' "Oriental Dyes."

Japan Floss. — Green — 512, 513, 513½, 514, 515. Brown—229, 230, 230½, 230¾, 230E. Pink—4, 6, 8, 8½, 10, 10½, 011, 013, 015 017. Yellow—647.

Turkish Floss.—White—691 for buttonhole scallop.

The basket of cherries illustrated at Color Plate No. 2 is a detail from centerpiece design 2921c, and in it the fruit is delightfully rendered as well as the basket which likewise exemplifies an excellent method of procedure. In the latter the rim and handle are first cotton filled and then worked solid in tan shade 229 of M. Heminway & Sons' Japan Floss. Over this is a strapping of brown 230E, which gives the twisted effect of the real basket. Graduated cat-stitch in alternating rows of 229 and 230 fills in the spaces between the basket ribs. Each time the stitches cross in the cat-stitch, they are couched lengthwise with a short stitch of the same color. For the basket ribs use two rows of outline stitch, one of light and one of dark brown, and 230½ may be added to the above mentioned in giving proper shading.

The cherries may or may not be filled—though raised cherries are more attractive. Kensington stitch is used, the stitches running from top to stem. The lightest ones, notably the one at top and directly under the handle, and the lightest ones hanging over the rim, are worked with pink 4, 6 and 8. That a touch of yellow may be sparingly introduced, is illustrated by the top cherry directly under the handle, which shows a few stitches of 647. Shades 8½, 10, 10½ and 011 appear in the slightly riper fruit, for which 013, 015 and 017 are used in varying quantities, and the deeper shades of dead ripe fruit are to be depicted through 011, 013 and 017. Skilful arrangement of color is largely a matter of judgment and memory, and the manifold tints of nature make it hard to go far astray. The main point is to keep the fruit properly modelled, that is, to study the light and shade, and blending of tint, that the cherries will appear round and without abrupt contrasts—they must never look spotted. Leaves are worked in Kensington; the stitches close laid, pointing from margin to midrib, are also worked with a single strand of Japan Floss. The lightest leaf, which falls over the basket rim, shows a tip and light section at the left of the midrib, executed in pale green 512 and 513 is worked into this while the veining is carried out in 514. A darker leaf is tipped with 513½, shaded into 514 and 515, and touches of brown 230¾ appear in the veining. Along the midrib and margin are a few stitches of 230 and 230½.

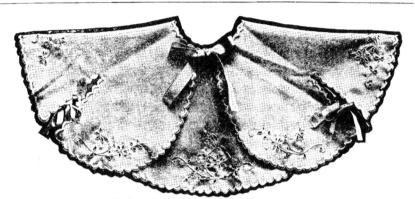

Infant's Embroidered Kimono.

DESIGN NO. 2400E.

This dainty adjunct to baby's wardrobe is stamped in one piece on French Finette, a superior quality of cream colored material resembling fine cashmere, by experience found to be the most appropriate for infant's wear.   It can be had in two lengths and sizes, large and small, and stamped in the following designs: daisies, wild roses, forget-me-nots, and eyelet, or just a plain scalloped edge without any flowers.   It is very effective, embroidered in white or colors, with Heminway Japan or Spanish Floss, and Turkish Floss for the scallops.

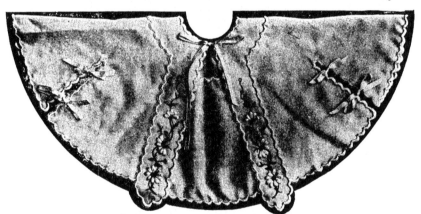

Infant's Embroidered Kimono.

DESIGN NO. 3000/2.

This style Kimono (small size only,) stamped on French Finette, can be obtained in another design (3000/1) which differs only in the collar.   A spray of small white daisies is placed where the dots with featherstitch lines appear.

Dealers' prices: small size, 60c.; large size, 75c.

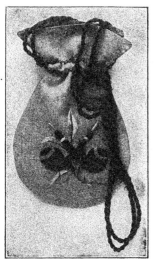

NO. 203/C.

Tobacco Pouch.

An appropriate gift of simple construction **for** the smoker. The foundation is gray homespun linen stamped in three different designs. Neatly stitch the sides. The bag to be lined with oil silk or colored cambric. The twisted cord is made of shades of brown and red Rope Silk, that blend with the shades of Brown Turkish Floss used in pipes. For the pipes use Japan Floss 548-623 dark brown, with a little of 622 light brown in the middle of bowl to give high light.

Use Old Gold No. 0409 for the mouth piece and rim of the bowl.

American Beauty Rose.

Design No. 2860 D. R.

Dealers in M. Heminway & Sons' Wash Silks can supply many handsome showpiece designs stamped on white linen, suitable for embroidering in Japan Floss and framing.

Flower and fruit subjects in vases, boxes and baskets.

2860DR.

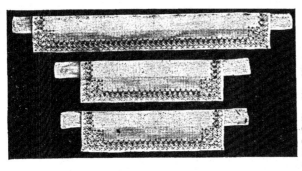

Collar and Cuffs on Dimity.

Width, 2 inches.
Length Collar, 12½ inches.
Length Cuffs, 7½ inches.

This illustration is a simple suggestion in Cross-stitch work, executed on checked dimity. The little square checks in the dimity material insure a safe guide for making the stitches even. Ornament with French knots, work both stitches with Turkish Floss. For outside row of Cross-stitches use Light Blue No. 564½, for the middle row use No. 565 lighter Blue, and for the inside row use Maize Yellow No. 409½.

The French knots (see page 21) are made in Black alternated with No. 409 Old Gold color and placed in the spaces between the Cross-stitches.

This set is very attractive worked as described and is equally pretty, though more modest, executed in Black and White Turkish Floss.

SCRIM WORK BAG.

Scrim Work Bag.

The illustration shows so clearly the style of construction, that little more can be said: No design is stamped on the material. The model is made of ordinary scrim—cut size 11½ x 17—folded over from bottom and seamed at sides, lined at top above the ribbons with colored china silk. The feather stitching is done with Oriental Dyes Rope Silk, two shades—old blue No. 293—Maize 0409.

The silk stitching is done after drawing two or three threads of scrim, then skipping five or six threads, again drawing two for the next row of silk stitches.

Round Pincushion.

A variety of designs can be obtained in size to fit a round 6-inch form cushion.

The top and bottom pieces are made large enough to permit of ribbon lacing, so they can be easily detached and cleaned.

ROUND PIN CUSHION, NO. 230/1.

Hat Pin Case.

Stamped in simple graceful sprays on white linen.

Fold the material twice and insert a piece of eiderdown in which the pins are inserted.

Secure with ribbon, in a color that will harmonize with the silk embroidery.

HOLLY, NO. 233/1.

GRASS, NO. 233/4.

Babies' Booties.

These practical little foot warmers are of very simple construction, stamped in three designs:

> Forget-Me-Not,
> Daisies,
> Wild Roses,

on fleeced pique.

The pattern for cutting is plainly stamped on the material. Bind with narrow ribbon, which also use for securing the uppers to the sole.

BABIES' BOOTIES.   NO. 236/1.

BOOTIES.   NO. 632.

Infants Booties stamped on heavy cricketers flannel in five parts, stitch the parts together with sewing cotton, matching the lines as stamped and ornament the seams with pink, light blue or cream twisted Embroidery Silk, feathered stitched. The top and flap to be button-holed. Finish with baby ribbon same color as the silk.

Infant's Bib.

Infants bib stamped on fine linen. The accompanying design—forget-me-not—embroidered in solid Kensington stitch with Japan Floss. Blues—564½, 564, 563½. Leaves, 437, 438, 439. Scollop buttonholed with white No. 691 Turkish Floss. Featherstitched at neck opening with white Spanish Floss.

Dainty lace for trimming.

This style bib, and larger size—similar style on Pique—can be obtained in two simple eyelet designs suitable for Spanish Floss work.

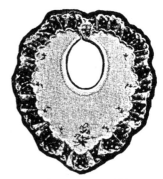

INFANT'S BIB NO. 218/2.

Glove and Handkerchief Cases.

GLOVE CASE. NO. 231/2.

HANDKERCHIEF CASE. NO. 232/4.

The two cases shown for gloves and handkerchiefs are made up in exactly the same way—by folding over once and lining with silk in color that will harmonize with the colors used in the silk embroidery. Pad with cotton containing a very little dainty perfumed powder.

Can be obtained in a variety of designs with scallop edge all around.

Tea Pot Holder.

A variety of designs stamped on white linen size about seven inches wide. To be lined with felt or flannel and trimmed with ribbon bow.

NO. 658.

Jewel Bags.

With Chamois Pockets.

Size about 4½ inches wide.

This useful novelty can be obtained in a variety of flower designs stamped on white linen. A complete neatly stitched chamois bag furnished with the stamped linens.

NO. 234/I.

NO. 2871/A.

Powder Sachet.

Furnished stamped on white linen in a variety of designs, size 4½ inches wide without the lace.

A silk sachet perfumed bag furnished with the stamped linens.

NO. 235/I.

N. B.—Other "Heminway" novelties that can be supplied by dealers, stamped and finished, are: Comb and Brush Cases, Hair Receivers, White and Tan Belts, Caps on French Finette and on Linen; Hair Pin Cases, Needle Books and Tea Cozys.

NO. 774J.

Shaving Paper Pad.

Diameter—9 inches.

Stamped on heavy tan material and furnished with tissue papers attached with eyelets to heavy cardboard.

This novelty can be obtained in several designs entitled:
"A Little Shaver,"
"A Daisy Shave,"
"Getting Out of a Bad Scrape,"
"A Daily Reminder."

Turkish Floss is the proper silk to use, button hole edge and finish with ribbon hanger selecting a color that will not clash with colors used in the embroidery.

Sample Card of Colored Floss.

Ladies will find it a convenience to have one of the elaborate color cards of Japan Floss showing 400 shades of the silk itself and containing samples of each kind of silk mentioned in the embroidery section of this book.

This card can be obtained of dealers. Price 10c. (which is less than actual cost), or will be mailed by the manufacturers of Japan Floss for 12c.

M. HEMINWAY & SONS' SILK CO.,
Watertown, Conn.

Illustrated Directions

FOR MAKING

FOUR-IN-HAND SCARF TIES

ADAPTED TO THE USE OF

M. HEMINWAY & SONS' PURE DYE
CROCHET SILK.

For smoothness of thread, uniformity of size and high lustre, this silk has no equal.

Purchasers will notice firm name, "M. Heminway & Sons," on every spool also red printed label. Every spool guaranteed full weight half ounce.

The Oriental dyes used in the process of dyeing this silk, are the same as used in the celebrated wash silks for embroidery, bearing same name.

Mills established more than half a century at Watertown, Conn.

Auto Scarf.

BASKET STITCH DESIGN

Abbreviations: k., knit; p., purl.

Knitted with M. Heminway & Sons' Crochet Silk, in any color desired, and a pair of No. 13 knitting needles, which may be either steel or bone. This scarf measures about 10 inches wide, and nearly 2 yards long, and will need six or eight balls of silk.

The Basket Stitch Pattern is worked upon any number of stitches, divisible by ten, with five over for the margin; therefore 95 stitches, or 105 stitches, may be cast on for the width of the scarf. Purl a row upon the cast-on stitches.

First Pattern Row.—P. 6, * k. 3, p. 7; repeat from *, and at the end k. 3 and p. 6.

Second Row.—K. 6, * p. 3, k. 7; repeat from *, and at the end p. 3 and p. 6.

Third Row—As the first row.

Fourth Row.—Purl all.

Fifth Row.—K. 4, * p. 7, k. 3; repeat from *; at the end knit the one last stitch.

Sixth Row.—P. 4, * k. 7, p. 3; repeat from *, and end by purling the one last stitch.

Seventh Row.—As fifth row.

Eighth Row.—Purl all.

Repeat these eight rows for the required length of the scarf, and cast off loosely.

The ends of the scarf are to be finished with a knotted fringe.

Crochet Silk Colors

A great variety of shades are made in M. Heminway & Son's Crochet Silk. All shades of Blue from the palest Baby Blue to dark Navy Blue, Gendarme, Alice Blue, Scarlet, Cardinal, Garnet, Wine, Plum, Heliotrope, Lavender, Corn, Gold, Orange, Rose, Pink, Shrimp, Castor, Pongee, Gray, Slate, Browns, Olive, Reseda, Myrtle and Nile Green. Old Gold, Black, White and Cream.

All spools guaranteed to contain full weight half ounce.

Scarf Tie Knitted in Brioche Stitch.

Materials Required. — Three spools of M. Heminway & Sons' Pure Dye Crochet Silk. One pair No. 22 Steel Knitting Needles.

Cast on 34 stitches, working as tightly as possible.

First Row.—Thread over needle and slip one as though to purl, knit one, and repeat to end of row.

Second Row.—Thread over needle and slip one as though to purl, knit together the next stitch and the thread which lies over it, and repeat to end.

Repeat the 2nd row until the work is 20 inches long.

Next Row.—Knit one, knit two together (the thread and the stitch) and repeat to end.

Second Neck Row.—Knit two, then knit two stitches together throughout the remainder of the row. Eighteen stitches will remain on the needle.

Knit one and purl one on these 18 stitches for a length of 16 inches, then widen for the second end of the tie, as follows:

Knit two, then knit two in each stitch throughout the remainder of the row. Next row work as with 1st row of tie, then proceed as with 2nd row until this end is 13 inches long. Bind off.

Crochet "Four-in-Hand" Necktie.

Materials.—Three spools of M. Heminway & Sons' Pure Dye Crochet Silk No. 1 or 2 Crochet Hook.

Directions for Making—(As Illustrated.)

CHAIN 21.

First Row.—Skip 2 chains and in the 3rd make 3 double crochets. Chain 1, again a double crochet in same chain. Repeat from *. When finished the row will contain 7 shells.

Second Row.—Turn, chain 3, * 3 double crochet over chain of one in first shell below, chain 1, 1 double crochet in same space. Repeat from * in each shell of 1st row. Repeat the 2nd row until the work is 14 inches long.

Next Two Rows.—Narrow 1 shell at each end of each row, when 3 shells will remain. In this width continue until the strip 3 shells wide is nineteen inches long.

Knitted "Four-in-Hand" Necktie.

Not illustrated.

Materials—Four Spools M. Heminway & Sons' Pure Dye Crochet Silk Four Steel Needles No. 17 or 18.

Cast on 56 stitches, 20 on one needle and 18 on two. Knit round and round for 7 inches. For the next round decrease 1 stitch at the beginning of the first needle and that of the third needle, and continue to decrease thus in every alternate round until there are only 28 stitches left. (Keep the second needle for the front of the tie.)

With 28 stitches on the needle, knit 14 inches, increase in the same order as decreasing is done, until there are 56 stitches on the needle.

Knit 14 in. and sew up the ends.

Crocheted Suspenders.

AS ILLUSTRATED.

Materials—Four spools Heminway & Sons pure dye Crochet Silk; chain 28 stitches, turn, and 3 d. c. in 4th stitch of chain, counting from the hook; 4 d. c. in 8th stitch of chain, 4 d. c. in 12th stitch of chain, and continue making 7 shells; second row, turn, chain 3 and 3 d. c. between first and second stitches of the last shell made; then 4 d. c. between first two stitches of next shell, and continue to end of row. Each succeeding row make like second row; make each suspender twenty-seven inches long and narrow down to one shell for the point.

The work should be done tight, or it will be necessary to line the suspender with ribbon.

Crocheted Suspenders.

STYLE B—COLORS GARNET AND BLACK.

Materials—M. Heminway & Sons pure dye Crochet Silk.

Make a chain of 150 stitches, garnet color, turn, 1st row, with the same color as the chain, miss 1 stitch, * 1 d. c. in the next, 1 chain; repeat from * to end of row; turn; 2d row, 1 chain, * 1 d. c. under the 1 chain of previous row, 1 chain; repeat from * to end of row; turn; 3d row, join on the black, and work 2 rows like the 2d. Continue repeating this 2d row until there are 22 rows in all, 2 rows of each color. The edge rows must be alike in color when finished, the lengths of silk left at the end of the rows must be neatly run in, and kid brace ends—that can be purchased ready made—are to be stitched on firmly with the silk.

See page 86 for list of shades that can be obtained in M. Heminway & Sons Crochet Silk.

Bedroom Slippers.

Quantity required, three spools of Heminway's Crochet Silk.

Cast on 19 or 21 stitches, according to size of slipper you wish to make. For a No. 4 slipper cast on 19 stitches and crochet 1 row plain.

Second row—crochet one bead with every stitch and add one in the centre of every row; third row—crochet plain, but still add a stitch in centre of row; fourth row is worked in the same way as second row. Continue to put in beads until you have about six or seven rows of them, then keep on crocheting with silk for about thirty-eight rows, which will make the front of slipper fifty rows in all, forming twenty-five ribs.

For the sides crochet 27 stitches, for sixty-eight rows, forming thirty-four ribs on each side of slipper and join them in the back. As a trimming for the top, crochet the following edging: First row—2 double stitches, one chain, 1 double stitch, 1 chain, and repeat. Second row—1 double stitch between the first 2 double stitches of first row; then 2 double stitches, 1 chain, 2 double stitches; in the next 1 double stitch and repeat. Third row—1 single stitch, 4 double, with 3 chains between each, and repeat. Then crochet the same lace again, let it fall downward and run a ribbon through the centre.

Crocheted Sailor's Knot Tie.

The materials required are two spools of M. Heminway & Sons crochet silk, one crochet needle, No. 3. Make a chain of 21, turn, and into 2d from needle work 1 single work 1 single into each of next two, and one treble into each of next three; end with 3 single. Turn with 3 chain, and into 1st stitch work 1 T, 1 T into next, and 3 single into next three stitches. This brings the trebles over the singles of last row and the singles over the trebles; repeat these rows until there are 12 inches worked. Then to decrease for the neck work in the row that begins with 3 treble, 3 chain to turn, miss 1 and work 1 T; work as usual to end of row, miss 1 stitch also at end. Decrease thus until there are 9 stitches left; work on these 9 for neck 15 inches (when the work is stretched), and increase again for the other end by working 4 treble in the first group of trebles, instead of 3, and increase at end of row also, then in the next row beginning with 4 treble, work 5 treble, and increase at the end. Then work 3 treble and 3 single in the next increasing row, and increase at end. Repeat the increasings until there are again 21 stitches. Work for 13 inches and finish off.—"Pictorial Review."

REFERENCE TABLE.

THE following reference table of shades in M. Heminway & Sons' "Oriental Dyes" Art Needlework Silks, has been prepared with care as a guide to embroiderers. The limited space will permit of only brief suggestions.

There is a difference of opinion regarding some flowers, but the following colors were selected with care and can be depended on as correct.

Flower	Color	Shades	Buds	Centres	Foliage
Acorn	Brown	301, 302, 303			370 to 374
Anemone	White	689, 691		649	428 to 430
	Pink	541 to 543		364	371 to 374
Apple Blossom	Pink	581 to 586	584, 585	647	572 to 574
Arbutus	Pink	581 to 583	583, 585	646	572 to 574
Aster	Violet	350 to 354	432	409	432 to 435
	Purple	557 to 561	371, 372	409	370 to 374
	Yellow	361 to 368	310½	409-410	310 to 313
	White	691	310	683-684	436 to 429½
	Pink	3 to 7	429, 430		428 to 431
Autumn Leaves	Terra Cotta				413 to 416
(Use natural leaves	Olive Browns				599 to 603
for models).	Golden "				0409 to 412
	Old Wood				526 to 530
	Tan Browns				390 to 394
	Tea Greens				437 to 439½
	Orange				653 to 654¾
	Dull Greens				678½ to 681
Azalea	White	691	395	364	371 to 374
	Dark Pink	581 to 585	584, 585	647	310½ to 313
	Clover Pink	540 to 544	543, 544	384	428 to 431
	Red	0655 to 658	658	662	436 to 439½
Bachelor Button	Blue	290 to 294	432, 433	432	432 to 435
or	"	260 to 263	429, 430	429	428 to 431
Begonia	White	691 & 370	371	648	0428 to 431
	Pink	404 to 406	406	647	371 to 374

Flower	Color	Shades	Buds	Centres	Foliage
Bluebell	Blue	260 to 263	373		371 to 374
Buttercup	Yellow	646 to 649	432	0432	432 to 434
Cactus	Red	011 to 015			371 to 375
	Yellow	649 to 653			370 to 375
California Pepper Berry	Red	638 to 642			310 to 313
Camellia	Pink	580 to 585			428 to 431
	Red	657 to 661			432 to 434
	White	689-691			436 to 439½
Canna	Yellow	647 to 654		651	437 to 439½
	Red	011 to 017		367	428 to 431
Carnation	Pink	1655 to 1661½	311, 312, 1657		310 to 313
	Red	011 to 017	372, 373, 13		371 to 374
	White	682 to 691	428, 429		428 to 431
	Old Pink	581 to 585	571, 572, 0582		570 to 573
	Shadow on				
	White	0682 to 683, 691			311 to 313
Cattails	Brown	302-303			683 to 686½
Chrysanthemum	Yellow	360 to 368	361, 363, 429		0428 to 430
	White	682-691	682, 438		436 to 439½
	Lavender	1475 to 1479	1477, 1479, 429		428 to 431
	Pink	0655 to 658	655, 657, 433		0432 to 434
	Dull Rose	404 to 406	0405, 406, 373		370 to 374
Cherry	Red	8 to 19	691, 682		310½ to 313
Clematis	Purple	350 to 355		432-433	0428 to 431
	White	691 & 371		778-780	370 to 374
.	Dull Purple	269 to 273			432 to 435
Clover	Pink	540 to 544		429	0432 to 434
	White and				
	Nile	691-0682, 682			0428 to 431
Columbine	Dull Lilac	270 to 273	272	310	311 to 313
	Pink	584 to 586	585	371	371 to 374
	Yellow	362 to 367	364	428	428 to 431
Cone (Pine)	Brown	301 to 304			
	Brown	392½ to 394			
Corn Flower	Blue	260 to 263	372, 373	236	371 to 374
Coreopsis	Yellow	646 to 649		300-302	371 to 374
Cosmos	Purple	1477 to 1481	311, 312, 1479	648-662	310½ to 312½
	Pink	541 to 543	372, 373, 542	647-662	371 to 374
	White	691-395-396	395, 827, 828	648-235	826 to 829
Coxcomb	Red	657 to 661			432 to 435
Crocus	Blue	565 to 563		367	371 to 374
	Purple	1477 to 1487		649	428 to 431
	Yellow	647 to 650		648	432 to 434
Cyclamen	White	689-436	436, 689, 438		437 to 439½
	Pink	383 to 387	384, 438		437 to 439½
Cypress	Pink	0655 to 658			371 to 374
Daffodil	Yellow	645 to 650	648, 649	648-312	310 to 313
Daisy	White	691-436	312	365	311 to 313
	Yellow	646 to 649	372	648	371 to 373
	Ox Eye	647 to 650	828	547-549	826 to 829
Dandelion	Yellow	647 to 649	372	365	371 to 374
Dogwood	White	691 0682-1655		428	0428 to 430
Fern	Maidenhair	0428 to 431		stems 236	

Flower	Color	Shades	Buds	Centres	Foliage
Fleur-de-lis or Iris	Purple	1475 to 1485	428, 429		0428 to 431
	Violet	461 to 464	372, 373		371 to 374
	Yellow	0645 to 647	433 434		432 to 435
Fleur-de-lis	Purple	460 to 464	481	648	395 to 399
	Purple	350 to 355	482		429 to 431½
Forget-me-not	Blue	565½ to 564½	582	647	436 to 439
Fuchsia	Red	8 to 15-691	11, 13, 428		0428 to 431
	Pink	1657 to 1661½	1659, 438, 439		436 to 439
	Purple	1479 to 1489	1481, 434, 435		432 to 435
Geranium	Pink	0582 to 585	583, 684	684	683 to 686
	Red	658 to 660	659, 312	312	310 to 313
	White	689-436	429, 430	429	428 to 431
Gladiolus	White	689-0682		647	436 to 439½
	Crimson	584 to 587		649	436 to 439½
	Red	2 to 15		648	0428 to 431
	Pink	581 to 585		647	0428 to 431
	Yellow	0645 to 649		648	432 to 435
	Purple	1477 to 1485		647	370 to 374
Golden Rod	Yellow	0645 to 650			0432 to 435
Grape	Ripe	590 to 593			
	Unripe	0682 to 684			0428 to 431
Hawthorn	White	691-0682			436 to 439
Heliotrope	Dull Purple	270 to 273	273	647	0428 to 430
	Lilac	590 to 593	593	648	0428 to 430
	White	689	689	647	436 to 439
Hibiscus	Old Rose	404 to 408			482 to 485
	Dull Pink	330 to 335			371 to 374
Holly	Red	013 to 017-690			826 to 829
Hollyhock	Nile	0682 to 683			684 to 687
	White	689-436-437	372, 373	371-648	370 to 374
	Pink	580 to 585	582, 429, 430	647-429	428 to 430
Honeysuckle	Pink	0655 to 656			428 to 430
	Gold Yellow	A645 to 646			436 to 439
	Old Red	532 to 535			371 to 374
Hops	Green	0428 to 429			432 to 435
Hyacinth	Pink	581 to 584	372		370 to 374
	Purple	558 to 561	429		428 to 431
	White	691-682	429		428 to 431
Hydrangia	Pink	581 to 585	372		371 to 374
	Pink	540 to 544	372		428 to 431
Jasmine (Cape)	Yellow	A645 to 648		0432	428 to 431
" (Star)	White	691-436		645	432 to 434
Jonquil	Yellow	362 to 364-691		372	370 to 374
Laurel	Pink	1657 to 1661½	1661		370 to 374
Lilac	Lilac	590 to 593	584, 591	647	370 to 374
	White	688	688	647	428 to 430
Lily, Tiger		657 to 662	371, 372, 373	649-690	370 to 374
Japanese	Pink	1657 to 1663	429, 430	648-662	428 to 431
Easter	White	395-396-397, 691	437, 438		436 to 439
Calla	White	689, 0682, 682	311, 312	648	310½ to 313
Pond	White	682-691	682, 372, 373	647	370 to 374
"	Pink	1657 to 1661	1659, 429, 430	648	428 to 431
Lily of the Valley	White	691, 682	310	310	310½ to 313

Flower	Color	Shades	Buds	Centres	Foliage
Magnolia	Pink	404-330 to 332	429, 430	0428	0428 to 431
	White	688-691-0682	429, 430	0428	0428 to 431
Marigold	Yellow	647 to 653	432, 433		432 to 434
	Red	659 to 662	827, 828		826 to 829
Mistletoe	Sage	395-396			436 to 439
Mignonette	Red & Green	300-301-428	429	645	0428 to 431
Morning Glory	Blue	565½ to 562	565, 564		371 to 374
	Purple	550 to 554	550, 552		432 to 435
	Pink	1657 to 1661½	1657, 1661		0428 to 431
Narcissus	White	691-0682-682	691, 682	647-609	370 to 374
	Yellow	0645 to 648		429	0428 to 431
Nasturtium	Orange	649 to 651	649, 651	236	436 to 439½
	Red	605 to 609	606, 608	645	0428 to 431
	Yellow	360 to 368	361, 363	236	678 to 680
Orange Blossom	White	682, 691	691	365-366	0428 to 431
Orchid	Purple	1475 to 1481	1477, 1481, 370	648-372	370 to 374
	Crimson	584 to 587	584, 585, 0432		0432 to 435
	Yellow	361 to 368	361, 363, 0428		0428 to 431
	Pink	540 to 545	540, 541, 0428	0409-429	0428 to 431
	Lilac	550 to 553	550, 551, 370	648-372	370 to 374
	Nile	395 to 397 & 691	691, 395	648-438	436 to 439½
Oxalia	White	691-310.	310	649, 651	437 to 439
	Pink	582 to 584	583	648	428 to 430
	Yellow	645 to 647	647	676	432 to 434
Pansy	Violet	350 to 354	351, 352	0409-429	0428 to 431
	Purple	460 to 464			0428 to 431
	Lilac	550 to 553	551, 552	367, 433	432 to 435
	Yellow	362 to 366	363, 365	409-373	371 to 374
	Old Rose	231 to 234	231, 232	368-373	371 to 574
Passion Flower	Purple	460 to 464		647	241 to 244
	Purple	1477 to 1487		364	371 to 374
Peony	Pink	541 to 543	372, 373		371 to 374
	Crimson	584 to 587	311, 312		310½ to 313
Phlox	Red	011 to 015			481 to 484
Poppy (California)	Orange	360 to 368	373, 372	367-372	370 to 373
" (Eastern)	Red	0655 to 662	659, 311, 312	647, 371-690	310½ to 313
Primrose	Pink	1655 to 1661	1657, 429	648-0428	428 to 431
	Purple	1477 to 1485	1481, 312	648-371	310½ to 313
	Yellow	360 to 367	363, 438	364-371	437 to 439½
Rainbow or Irridescent		682-1479-655-363 629			
Rhododendron	Pink	583 to 587			370 to 374
	Pink	540 to 543			370 to 374
Rose	Am. Beauty	381 to 389	383 to 387, 429, 430		0428 to 431
	Jacque	636 to 643	638 to 640, 429, 430		0428 to 431
	La France	580 to 585-682	0582 to 583, 372, 373		370 to 374
	Marechal Niel	360 to 368	{ 362, 363, 571, 572		570 to 573
	Wild	1657 to 1661	1561, 438, 439	438-647	436 to 439½

Flower	Color	Shades	Buds	Centres	Foliage
Rose	Tea	340 to 346	342 to 345, 438, 439		436 to 439½
Rose (Bride's)	Pink	580 to 583			571 to 573
Spirea	White	691-0428-0682			370 to 373
Strawberry	Red	0655 to 660		0432	
	Unripe	0428, 428			0432 to 435
	Flower	691-682	434	647	
Sumach	Berry	414 to 415¼			
	Flower	688, 691-0428			371 to 374
Sweet Pea	Dark Pink	584 to 586	585, 586, 373		370 to 373
	Shell Pink	A655 to 656	655, 656, 373		371 to 374
	White	688, 0682	682, 438.		437 to 439
	Purple	1475 to 1481	1477, 1479, 430		0428 to 431
	Violet	350 to 352	351. 352, 430		0428 to 431
	Lilac	550 to 552	551, 552, 438		437 to 439
	Red	8 to 17	11, 13, 372		371 to 373
Sweet William	Red	636 to 640	438	0428	436 to 439
	Pink	584 to 586	429	428	428 to 430
	White	691-436	438	645	436 to 439
Thistle	Purple	1479-1487	1485, 395, 398		395 to 399
	Lilac	590 to 593-580 to 582	592-370-372		370 to 373
Trumpet Vine	Red	525 to 527	526½, 372, 373		371 to 374
Tube Rose	White	688-0682	310½, 311		310½ to 313
Tulip	Red	638 to 642	372, 373, 639, 640	373	371 to 374
	Pink	581 to 584	429, 430, 0582 582	429	428 to 431
	Yellow	361 to 366	429, 430, 362, 363	429	428 to 431
	White	691-395	691, 436 to 438	437	436 to 439
Verbena	Light Pink	1655 to 1661		0428	428 to 431
	Purple	559 to 561		0432	432 to 435
	Red	013 to 017		0432	432 to 435
	Dark Pink	582 to 585		676	371 to 374
Violet	Single	350 to 355	352, 430	609-430	428 to 431
	Double	461 to 464	463, 433	609-433	432 to 434
	White	691-0682, 682 360-A408 to 408½	682, 373	609-373	371 to 374 428 to 431
Wheat					371 to 374
Wisteria	Purple	1475 to 1485	372 to 373		371 to 374
	White	691	433, 434		432 to 435

MISCELLANEOUS.

Flame	605 to 607, 280 to 285
Pine Cone	300 to 303
Pomegranite	232 to 0236
Palm	310½ to 313
Seaweed	300 to 303, 414 to 415¼, 370 to 374 679 to 681
Smilax	0428 to 430
Flag Blue	417
China Blue	290 to 294

MISCELLANEOUS—*Continued.*

Convention Designs	Blue, 671 to 673, 290 to 295
	Green, 371 to 374, 682 to 686½
	Browns, 390 to 394, 226 to 230F, 280 to 285, 0408 to 412
	Terra Cottas, 413 to 416
	Grey, 1196 to 1202
	Burnt Rose, 231 to 0236
Oriental Effects	520 to 523½, 599 to 603, 231 to 0236, 300 to 303, 570 to 573, 413 to 415¾, 280 to 285, 226 to 230D, 550 to 553, 670 to 673, 310 to 313. Outline around the embroidered scrolls with black silk or gold thread.

Rainbow	⎫ These effects can be produced on conventional designs by a com-
Opalescent	⎪ bination of the following shades: 682 Nile Green; 1657
Irridescent	⎬ Pale Pink; 0645 Canary; 1477 Lavender; 0408 Maize; 691
Sunshine	⎪ Pure White; 695 Turquois; 342 Tea Rose; 634 Nile Green.
Autumn Leaves	370 to 374, 231 to 0236, 300 to 303, 678 to 680, 413 to 415¾, 526 to 529

COLLEGE COLORS.

The shade numbers noted below are correct for the various Colleges mentioned, information having been obtained through correspondence.

Adelphi College	Brooklyn, N. Y.	Brown & Gold	548, 649
Amherst College	Amherst, Mass.	Purple & White	355, 691
Armour Inst. of Technology	Chicago, Ills.	Yellow & Black	648, 690
Boston University	Boston, Mass.	Scarlet & White	013, 691
Brown University	Providence, R. I.	Brown & White	549, 691
Columbia University	New York City	Lt. Blue & White	565, 691
Columbian University	Washington, D. C	Orange & Blue	368-417
Cornell University	Ithaca, N. Y.	Cardinal & White	015-691
Dartmouth College	Hanover, N. H.	Dark Green	"Dartmouth'
Dickinson College	Carlisle, Pa.	Cardinal & White	015-691
Girard College	Philadelphia, Pa.	Grey & Garnet	1200-021
Harvard University	Cambridge, Mass.	Crimson	588
Hobart College	Geneva, N. Y.	Crimson	588
Johns Hopkins University	Baltimore, Md.	Black & Blue	690-417
Lafayette College	Easton, Pa.	Garnet & White	021-691
Lehigh University	Bethlehem, Pa.	Brown & White	394-691
Mass. Institute Technology	Boston, Mass.	Cardinal & Grey	642-1200
Mercer University	Macon, Ga.	Orange & Black	652-690
Oberlin College	Oberlin, Ohio	Crimson & Gold	587-368
Packer Institute	Brooklyn, N. Y.	Garnet	021
Pratt Institute	Brooklyn, N. Y.	Yellow	366
Princeton University	Princeton, N. J.	Orange & Black	653-690
Smith College	Northampton, Mass.	White	691
Stanford University	Palto Alto, Cal.	Cardinal	015
Stevens Institute Technology	Hoboken, N. J.	Grey & Scarlet	1200 & 011
Syracuse University	Syracuse, N. Y.	Orange	653
Union College	Schenectady	Garnet	019
University of California	Berkeley, Cal.	Blue & Gold	417-367
University of Chicago	Chicago, Ills.	Maroon	021
University of Michigan	Ann Arbor	Maize & Blue	408½-564

COLLEGE COLORS—*Continued.*

Vassar College	Poughkeepsie	Light Gray and Rose	1196-582
Wellesley College	Wellesley, Mass.	Blue	562
Wesleyan University	Middletown, Ct.	Cardinal & Black	640-690
Williams College	Williamstown, Mass.	Royal Purple	353
Yale University	New Haven. Ct.	Blue	"Yale"

SUBLIME
Glove Mending
SILK.
M. HEMINWAY & SONS SILK CO.
25 COLORS.

ONE of the specialties made by M. Heminway & Sons Silk Co. is a sewing silk put up in convenient form, braided in needle lengths ready for use. It differs from the machine silk put up on spools, being two-ply reverse twist, and works smoother in hand work than does machine twist on spools, which is specially made for sewing machines.

Made in three assortments:

Assortment No. 1.—Dark staple shades, including Black.

Assortment No. 2.—Selected glove shades.

Assortment No. 3.—Bright fancy colors, including White.

Each braid contains 25 shades.

Total number of needle lengths 432.

Price, 30 cents, of dealers.

TABLE OF CONTENTS.

A SAFE HOBBY

AN article that can hold public favor for more than half a century, can be relied upon to give satisfaction to the most critical of the present generation. " When you use silk use <u>Good</u> Silk." The best stores offer you M. Heminway & Sons' "Sublime" Quality.

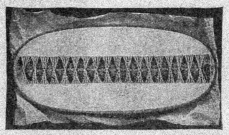

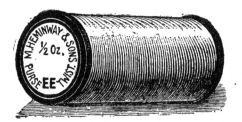

Illustrated instructions for making this handsome chatelaine bag and many others, as well as silk coin purses, watch pockets, etc., will be mailed to any address on receipt of 10c. in stamps.

Chatelaine Bag.

All the rules are applicable to our

MB 103.

Pure Dye

Purse Twist and Crochet Silk

See fac-simile of spools as sold by representative stores throughout the United States.

Women know!

It isn't necessary to tell *them* how to wash the thousand and one pretty trifles that come under the general name of "fancy work." They would not think of using ordinary laundry soap—or washing powders—or chemicals. Oh, no!

There is a better way; a safer way—Ivory Soap and lukewarm water.

Why Ivory Soap? Because it is pure; because it contains no "free" alkali; no coloring matter; no harmful ingredient of any kind.

"APPROVED METHODS FOR HOME LAUNDERING" is a substantial and intensely practical little book of 68 pages. The first chapter is devoted to an explanation of the value of laundry work, from the standpoint of health and comfort. Then follow chapters on Stains (with detailed directions for their removal), Fabrics, Soap, Laundry Aids, Laundry Equipment, Practical Laundry Work and Directions for Special Articles. The book is free. Write right away, if you would like a copy. THE PROCTER & GAMBLE CO , Cincinnati, Ohio.

Ivory Soap . . . . . 99$\frac{44}{100}$ Per Cent. Pure.

CPSIA information can be obtained
at www.ICGtesting.com
Printed in the USA
LVOW13s1507160517

534724LV00039B/1609/P